KUVASZ

A COMPLETE AND RELIABLE HANDBOOK

by Dana I. Alvi and Leslie Benis

RX-108

Title page: A pair of Kuvasz puppies owned by Karpati Kennels.

Photographers: Mary Bloom, Callea Photo, Richard Demay, Deb Eldredge, Dorie Engstrom, Isabelle Francais, Agi Hejja, Judy Iby, Linda Lloyd, Christina Manente, Terry Phillips, Vince Serbin, and Sally Anne Thompson.

© by T.F.H. Publications, Inc.

Distributed in the UNITED STATES to the Pet Trade by T.F.H. Publications, Inc., One T.F.H. Plaza, Neptune City, NJ 07753; distributed in the UNITED STATES to the Bookstore and Library Trade by National Book Network, Inc. 4720 Boston Way, Lanham MD 20706; in CANADA to the Pet Trade by H & L Pet Supplies Inc., 27 Kingston Crescent, Kitchener, Ontario N2B 2T6; Rolf C. Hagen Inc., 3225 Sartelon St. Laurent-Montreal Quebec H4R 1E8; in CANADA to the Book Trade by Vanwell Publishing Ltd., 1 Northrup Crescent, St. Catharines, Ontario L2M 6P5 ; in ENGLAND by T.F.H. Publications, PO Box 15, Waterlooville PO7 6BQ; in AUSTRALIA AND THE SOUTH PACIFIC by T.F.H. (Australia), Pty. Ltd., Box 149, Brookvale 2100 N.S.W., Australia; in NEW ZEALAND by Brooklands Aquarium Ltd. 5 McGiven Drive, New Plymouth, RD1 New Zealand; in Japan by T.F.H. Publications, Japan—Jiro Tsuda, 10-12-3 Ohjidai, Sakura, Chiba 285, Japan; in SOUTH AFRICA by Lopis (Pty) Ltd., P.O. Box 39127, Booysens, 2016, Johannesburg, South Africa. Published by T.F.H. Publications, Inc.

MANUFACTURED IN THE
UNITED STATES OF AMERICA
BY T.F.H. PUBLICATIONS, INC.

CONTENTS

DESCRIPTION
OF THE KUVASZ

TEMPERAMENT

It is not surprising that the Kuvasz was the first of the three ancient Hungarian herding breeds to find his way into the cities and suburbs adapting himself to modern-day living. A spirited dog, wholeheartedly devoted, fanatically loyal with plenty of self determination, courage, and curiosity, he was used for centuries as a guard and companion dog earning the respect and love of all those who shared their lives with him. The Kuvasz is proven to be fearless in his guarding duty and is a rugged working dog capable of adjusting to extreme climates and conditions.

Whereas young dogs have a sense of humor and stay clowns for a long time, the grown Kuvasz is quiet

The Kuvasz is the most ancient of the three Hungarian herding breeds, and the herding instinct remains strong in the breed today. Here Deb Eldredge and Bubba are working sheep.

The modern Kuvasz is a rugged working dog whose greatest need is sharing activities with his owner.

and dignified, barking only when necessary. Though not a fighter, he will stand up to any foe. He is always alert and is able to move with lightning speed if necessary.

Apart from the basic physical requirements of food and reasonable shelter, his greatest need is the sharing of each day's activities with his human family or having a responsibility, such as guarding his home,

The Kuvasz has proven to be fearless in his guarding duty, especially when it comes to his home. This confident dog is protecting his owners' flower bed.

DESCRIPTION

watching over children or helping with livestock. Constant inactivity, or kennel life, is definitely not for a Kuvasz. Basically, he is a one family dog. Given the chance, he seems to prefer the company of children. He likes to be near them and is gentle but ready and willing to accept an invitation to play. Being very sensitive, the mature dog is able to judge the intensity of his play. Moments after lively "wrestling" with older children, the same dog will quietly accept the affections of a crawling infant. The play of puppies and young children should be supervised as neither seem to know the limit. It is of great importance that parents educate their small children in the care of a dog and teach them the difference between a stuffed toy and a live animal whose feelings of pain and pleasure must be recognized.

Towards accepted strangers, the Kuvasz is polite but rather suspicious and very discriminating in making new friends.

Opposite: The Kuvasz is a large spirited dog who is wholeheartedly devoted to his human family. Owner, Karpati Kennels.

The Kuvasz seems to prefer the company of children; he is gentle and ready and willing to play. Puppies and children should always be supervised, as neither seem to know the limit. Owner, Deb Eldredge.

The head of the Kuvasz is considered to be his most attractive feature. It should show harmony, gentleness, and a kindly intelligent expression.

APPEARANCE

Being a working dog of large size, the Kuvasz is well proportioned; sturdily built with excellent balance; strong boned; well muscled, but not coarse under any circumstances. His impressive strength and tireless activity combined with graceful light-footedness compose unsurpassed beauty and elegance. Among dog breeds tendency to weakness or lack of substance is considered a serious fault. In judging the Kuvasz, it is most important to pay attention to the balance of substance and graceful movement. Front and hindquarters are well developed to assure elastic and rhythmic movement on strong legs. Dogs with signs of unsound hips, straight stifles or cowhocked legs should not be considered for exhibition or breeding purposes.

The conscientious breeders pay attention to the finer details of quality in their effort to preserve correct type and beauty. They consider the head of the Kuvasz to be his most attractive feature. It should show harmony, gentleness, kindly expression combined with intelligence. The skull is oblongated but not pointed, with a long, slightly domed forehead. The ideal length of the head is 45% of the dog's height at the top of the shoulders. The width of the head is half of its length. The top of the muzzle is straight, and it connects with the forehead with a not-too-pronounced stop. Its length is less than half (42%) of the length of the head. The "V" shaped ears measure 50% of the length of the head, stand slightly away from the head in the upper part, then lie close to it. The scissors bite is ideal, and the level bite is acceptable. Flews are tight and black, even the slightest droopiness here is considered faulty. The length of his body forms a horizontal rectangle only slightly deviated from the square.

Another characteristic feature of the Kuvasz is the profusely coated low-set tail that, with the exception of the end curl, never rises above the topline. Owner, Dorie Engstrom.

The medium length, well-muscled neck flows into the chest without dewlap. The other characteristic

feature of the breed is the profusely-coated, low-set tail that, with the exception of the end curl, never rises above the topline. The lower third of the tail can bend upward, but it should never curl over the back or "corkscrew" over the loin.

The Kuvasz moves like a wolf, with much agility, freedom, ease, elasticity and light-footedness. His gait is powerful, outreaching, graceful and rhythmic without any side swing of the legs and body. His feet travel close to the ground, and as the speed increases they angle under the center line of the body, almost single tracking. At a trot and fast gallop, the Kuvasz seems to glide with minimal up and down movement of the body. This effortless movement makes him capable of trotting 15 to 18 miles without tiring; this desired graceful, rhythmic movement cannot be maintained without sufficient angulation and firm slimness of the body.

Opposite: Sufficiently exercising your Kuvasz on rough ground will wear his nails down, keeping his "cat like" feet tight. Owner, Nola Stevens.

Although size is quite desirable, bulkiness, excess weight, coarseness of bone and head structure are most undesirable. A 28-inch male Kuvasz should weigh around one hundred pounds, a 26-inch female around 75 pounds.

Perhaps the most amazing characteristic of this white dog is the frequent occurrence of litters whelped with complete black pigmentation on skin, eye lids, nose, lips and nails. From the standpoint of pigmentation, such puppies are the most desirable for the consideration of their use as breeding stock.

The Kuvasz that is sufficiently exercised on rough ground wears his nails down keeping his "cat like" feet tight. The amount of excess nail that has to be trimmed off by the owner indicates the amount of needed exercise the dog did not receive.

The most amazing characteristic of the Kuvasz is the frequent occurrence of litters born with complete black skin pigmentation. Note the black noses on these young puppies bred by Linda Lloyd.

OFFICIAL STANDARD FOR THE KUVASZ

The following standard is the approved standard of the American Kennel Club, the principal governing body for the dog sport in the United States.

General Appearance—A working dog of larger size, sturdily built, well balanced, neither lanky nor cobby. White in color with no markings. Medium boned, well muscled, without the slightest hint of bulkiness or lethargy. Impresses the eye with strength and activity combined with light-footedness, moves freely on strong legs. The following description is that of the ideal Kuvasz. Any deviation must be penalized to the extent of the deviation.

Size, Proportion, Substance—*Height* measured at the withers: Dogs, 28 to 30 inches; bitches, 26 to 28 inches. *Disqualifications:* Dogs smaller than 26 inches. Bitches smaller than 24 inches. *Weight:* Dogs approximately 100 to 115 pounds, bitches approxi-

Kuvaszok are large working dogs measuring from 26 to 30 inches at the shoulder and weighing from 70 to 115 pounds.

mately 70 to 90 pounds. Trunk and limbs form a horizontal rectangle slightly deviated from the square. *Bone* in proportion to size of body. Medium, hard. Never heavy or coarse. Any tendency to weakness or lack of substance is a decided fault.

Head—Proportions are of great importance as the head is considered to be the most beautiful part of the Kuvasz. Length of head measured from tip of nose to occiput is slightly less than half the height of the dog at the withers. Width is half the length of the head. *Eyes* almond-shaped, set well apart, somewhat slanted. In profile, the eyes are set slightly below the plane of the muzzle. Lids tight, haws should not show. Dark brown, the darker the better. *Ears* V-shaped, tip is slightly rounded. Rather thick, they are well set back between the level of the eye and the top of the head. When pulled forward the tip of the ear should cover the eye. Looking at the dog face to face, the widest part of the ear is about level to the eye. The inner edge

AmCan. Ch. Czigany Abracadabra, CGC, owned by Linda Lloyd, wins Best of Breed at the Kuvasz Club of America's first National Specialty Show in Reno, Nevada, in 1993.

The ears of the Kuvasz are V-shaped and the tips are slightly rounded. Rather thick, they are well set back between the level of the eye and the top of the head. Owner, Carol A. Nock.

of the ear lies close to the cheek, the outer edge slightly away from the head forming a V. In the relaxed position, the ears should hold their set and not cast backward. The ears should not protrude above the head. The *skull* is elongated but not pointed. The stop is defined, never abrupt, raising the forehead gently above the plane of the muzzle. The longitudinal midline of the forehead is pronounced, widening as it slopes to the muzzle. Cheeks flat, bony arches above the eyes. The skin is dry. *Muzzle:* length in proportion to the length of the head, top straight, not pointed, underjaw well developed. Inside of the mouth preferably black. *Nose* large, black nostrils well opened. *Lips* black, closely covering the teeth. The upper lip covers tightly the upper jaw only; no excess flews. Lower lip tight and not pendulous. *Bite*: dentition full, scissors bite preferred. Level bite acceptable. *Disqualifications*: overshot bite; undershot bite.

Neck, Topline, Body—*Neck* muscular, without dewlap, medium length, arched at the crest. *Back* is of medium length, straight, firm and quite broad. The loin is short, muscular and tight. The croup well muscled, slightly sloping. Forechest is well devel-

The Kuvasz's back is of medium length, straight, firm and quite broad.

oped. When viewed from the side, the forechest protrudes slightly in front of the shoulders. Chest deep with long, well-sprung ribs reaching almost to the elbows. The brisket is deep, well developed and runs parallel to the ground. The stomach is well tucked up. *Tail* carried low, natural length reaching at least to the hocks. In repose it hangs down resting on the body, the end but slightly lifted. In state of excitement, the tail may be elevated to the level of the loin, the tip slightly curved up. Ideally there should not be much difference in the carriage of the tail in state of excitement or in repose.

Forequarters—Shoulders muscular and long. Topline—withers are higher than the back. The scapula and humerus form a right angle, are long and of equal length. Elbows neither in nor out. Legs are medium boned, straight and well muscled. The joints are dry, hard. Dewclaws on the forelegs should not be removed. *Feet* well padded. Pads resilient, black. Feet are closed tight, forming round "cat feet." Some hair between the toes, the less the better. Dark nails are preferred.

Hindquarters—The portion behind the hip joint is moderately long, producing wide, long and strong muscles of the upper thigh. The femur is long, creating well-bent stifles. Lower thigh is long, dry, well muscled. Metatarsus is short, broad and of great strength. Dewclaws, if any, are removed. Feet as in front, except the rear paws somewhat longer.

Coat—The Kuvasz has a double coat, formed by guard hair and fine undercoat. The texture of the coat is medium coarse. The coat ranges from quite wavy to straight. Distribution follows a definite pattern over

The back of the forelegs are feathered with hair 2 to 3 inches long, and the back of the thighs and the tail are covered with hair 4 to 6 inches long. Owner, Anthony M. Pauldine.

The Kuvasz's head, muzzle and ears are covered with short smooth hair. The neck has a mane that extends to and covers the chest.

the body regardless of coat type. The head, muzzle, ears and paws are covered with short, smooth hair. The neck has a mane that extends to and covers the chest. Coat on the front of the forelegs up to the elbows and the hind legs below the thighs is short and smooth. The backs of the forelegs are feathered to the pastern with hair 2 to 3 inches long. The body and sides of the thighs are covered with a medium length coat. The back of the thighs and the entire tail are covered with hair 4 to 6 inches long. It is natural for the Kuvasz to lose most of the long coat during hot weather. Full luxuriant coat comes in seasonally, depending on climate. Summer coat should not be penalized.

Color—White. The skin is heavily pigmented. The more slate gray or black pigmentation the better. *Disqualification:* any color other than white.

Gait—Easy, free and elastic. Feet travel close to the ground. Hind legs reach far under, meeting or

The Kuvasz is always ready to protect loved ones, even to the point of self-sacrifice. Bubba gives up half of his bed for owner Tom Eldredge.

even passing the imprints of the front legs. Moving toward an observer, the front legs do not travel parallel to each other, but rather close together at the ground. When viewed from the rear, the hind legs (from the hip joint down) also move close to the ground. As speed increases, the legs gradually angle more inward until the pads are almost single-tracking. Unless excited, the head is carried rather low at the level of the shoulders. Desired movement cannot be maintained without sufficient angulation and firm slimness of body.

Temperament—A spirited dog of keen intelligence, determination, courage and curiosity. Very sensitive to praise and blame. Primarily a one-family dog. Devoted, gentle and patient without being overly

Kuvasok possess an untiring ability to work. These Kuvaszok show two youngsters the ropes of carting. Owner, Linda Lloyd.

demonstrative. Always ready to protect loved ones even to the point of self-sacrifice. Extremely strong instinct to protect children. Polite to accepted strangers, but rather suspicious and very discriminating in making new friends. Unexcelled guard, possessing ability to act on his own initiative at just the right moment without instruction. Bold, courageous and fearless. Untiring ability to work and cover rough terrain for long periods of time. Has good scent and has been used to hunt game.

DISQUALIFICATIONS

Overshot bite. Undershot bite.

Dogs smaller than 26 inches. Bitches smaller than 24 inches.

Any Color other than white.

Approved July 9, 1974

Reformatted March 28, 1991

The Kuvasz is devoted, gentle, and patient. Here Tom Eldredge and Bubba dress up as anesthesiologists for the Costume Class.

HISTORY OF THE KUVASZ

Many conjectured theories have evolved around the histories of the old breeds. Some claim antiquity and facts not authenticated by reliable evidence. For a long time, the history of the Hungarian working breeds was surrounded by many such speculations and their origin placed in vastly separated regions. In November 1965, the first monthly periodical entitled *The Puli* was published in the English language. Its author is the Hungarian-born kynologist, Sandor Palfalvy, MD, member of the Alabama Academy of Science. Dr. Palfalvy has bred the Puli for 47 years. Many of those years were spent in serious research delving into the history of his chosen breed. His inquiries led him to contact with other Hungarian scientists who fled their occupied country and in the free world were busily working on their old project, the origin of the Hungarian nation. This long research produced startling discoveries not only on the history of the Hungarian people, but also the background of the three Hungarian breeds, Kuvasz, Puli and Komondor, which until now was uncertain.

Dr. Palfalvy's and his colleagues' search included a thorough study of Sumerian, Sanskrit, Greek and Latin literature, as well as the study of the excavated findings of the Tigris-Euphrates Valley. They inform us that the names of the three breeds are frequently mentioned in the ancient literatures. Kuvasz, Puli and Komondor were domesticated and belonged to the Sumerian herdsmen dating back 7000–8000 years, and these breeds accompanied them during their travels from Mesopotamia to the Carpathian-encircled present-day Hungary.

The word Kuvasz (plural Kuvasok) is Sumerian. The first letters KU are from an old Sumerian word for dog, KUDDA. KUDDA is made up of two words:

The Puli, one of the three native breeds of Hungary, is a small herding dog that possesses a corded coat. Owner, Menth Lina.

KUN meaning tail and ADA meaning give. KUN-ADA: give the tail, the animal that gives the tail, that expresses itself with the tail. KUDDA later evolved into KUTTA and is used even today by people speaking the Dravidian languages whose ancestors fled Mesopotamia when it was conquered by the Assyrians. Modern Hungarian, a Sumerian language on a twen-

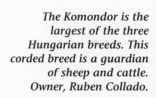

The Komondor is the largest of the three Hungarian breeds. This corded breed is a guardian of sheep and cattle. Owner, Ruben Collado.

tieth century level, has the word KUTYA. ASSA means horse in Sumerian. KU-ASSA was a dog that guarded and ran alongside horses and horsemen.

The Kuvasz is an ancient breed whose origins have been uncovered within the ruins of present-day Hungary.

In 1931, during explorations of the ruins of the 5000 BC city of Ugarit in Mesopotamia led by an English archeologist, Sir H.J. McDonald, a 7000-year-old clay tablet was found. Inscribed on it in cuneiform writing was the word KU-AS-SA. This tablet can now be viewed at the British Museum in London.

In the Oriental Museum of Paris, two clay boards are displayed that were found at the ruins of the city of Kish by a French archeologist, Maurice Espreaux. Both are inscribed in cuneiform with the word KU-AS-SA.

Also in Mesopotamia, by the river Euphrates, was a city called Ur that flourished during the 35th century BC. It is also mentioned in the Old Testament. Within its ruins, two clay boards were found that listed the belongings of two families, Kuth and Bana. Along with a number of horses, cattle and sheep there are listed Pulik, Komondorok and eight KU-AS-SA owned by the Kuth family and two by Bana. The excavations of the city of Ur were conducted by the British Academy of Science headed by Sir C. Leonard Wooley, archeologist. The boards are at the British Museum.

Still another clay board with cuneiform written KU-ASSA, now at the Asmolean Museum, was found at the site of Akkad, a Sumerian city of the 30th century BC in Northern Mesopotamia.

The great Babylonian king Hammurabi, 2250 BC, inscribed a series of laws on a huge stone now at the Louvre Museum in Paris. The Code of Hammurabi, as it is called, dictates almost all aspects of daily life. Included in the Code is the mention of the three Hungarian breeds by name, the Kuvasz, Komondor and Puli, unchanged for many thousands of years.

The Kuvasz originated as a Hungarian herding dog and many Kuvasok are still employed as herdsman today.

Of course, the experts on kynology could not find the origin of the words Kuvasz, Komondor and Puli, as their search was based on the Finno-Ugric theory that *originated* Hungarians in the Ural area of the Caucasus. Dr. Palfalvy's findings are not in opposition to the historical facts that Hungarians migrated to the present-day Hungary with their horses and dogs and sheep from the Ural area but take them back another 5000 years before that era.

The latter-day written evidences dating back as far as the 1400s seem to prove that the Kuvasz became the first Hungarian breed to follow his master into the homes and cities from the endless prairies. King Mathias' enthusiasm for this breed (around 1460) opened the doors for the Kuvasz among the nobility.

The horsemen and shepherds who bred the Kuvasz for thousands of years did not concern themselves with keeping pedigrees of their dogs. There was no real paper work as the dogs were not

Many well-known German, Swiss and Hungarian scientists credit the origin of the Great Pyrenees, shown here, from Kuvasz ancestors. Owner, June M. St. Onge.

At 14 weeks of age, Bubba learns to backpack with the hopes of visiting the mountainous region from which his ancestors came. Owner, Deb Eldredge.

permitted to mate unselected. The beginning of scientific breeding, and the time when strict breeding records were kept can be considered to have started from the late 1800s.

MODERN HISTORY

We have to mention here that well-known German, Swiss and Hungarian scientists credit the origin of the Great Pyrenees from Kuvasz ancestors, in opposition to the view of some dog writers of the 1950s. Just as one example, even in the 1960s, the Great Pyrenees breed club in West Germany is still a subchapter of the "Hungarian Herding Dogs Club." The Hungarian Herding Dog Breeders Association, since their first publications dating from the early 1920s, put much emphasis on working quality and set it as the number one goal for hobby breeders The Association's first president, Dr. Emil Rajtsits, put down the foundations to adapt the Hungarian herding breeds to the rapidly modernizing life in the 20th century. His work was a success and so encouraging that many dedicated kynologists and breeders joined him to achieve the goals he set. As a result, to breed or to own a Hungarian dog became a national pride in the Kuvasz's native country, and this in itself is the greatest assurance for the future of the breed.

In 1939, the Kuvasz became the fashion dog among the large breed enthusiasts in Hungary and Western Europe alike. This progress was greatly harmed by World War II. Dogs suffered from shortages of food and other essentials such as vitamins and medicines. Kennels voluntarily reduced their breeding stock to a minimum, individual owners were forced to give away their most valuable animals due to military duty and other wartime complications.

Faithful guard dogs were killed by the hundreds, first by the Germans, later by the Russian occupying forces in order to let them move freely on their ransacking missions.

The end of the war found the breed in a very sad state. Many Kuvasz fanciers were dead, most dogs had been destroyed or were missing. Numerous dogs were scattered all over Europe with their owners escaping before the Russian take-over. A new start could not be made immediately. For a long time mail service was unheard of, and it took years to measure up the extent of the loss. The occupying Russians and the new regime looked upon dog breeding as a luxury hobby of the aristocracy, and treated it accordingly. Nonetheless, as long as life goes on people have the desire to return to normal life and will make all the sacrifices for their strongest interest. In the post-war chaos, breeders met in secrecy to establish a direction to follow. The first puppies and dogs were sold for cigarettes, food and natural goods before currency stabilization.

The Kuvasz, like all other large breeds, suffered a setback in popularity because of the feeding difficulties compared to smaller dogs, and this situation held true until the 1956 Hungarian Revolution. Since then, the living standard improved to the point where the Kuvasz began to regain his pre-war popularity. During the period immediately following the war, living conditions in Western Europe improved at a much faster pace, and this helped the sport of dog breeding.

THE KUVASZ IN AMERICA

Like millions of other inhabitants of the United States, the Kuvasz, too, is an immigrant. A young pair was brought over in the late 1920s by a Hungarian couple seeking better living in the land of promise. As their initial years proved difficult, it became necessary to part with the animals. A Miss M.E. Marsh of Madison, New Jersey, who later became Mrs. J. Scoffield Rowe, being fascinated with the majestic beauty of the Kuvasz purchased the male. With much difficulty and expense, Mrs. Rowe imported a bitch and soon became the owner of the first American-bred litter of Kuvaszok, establishing the Romanse Kennels.

In 1931, the American Kennel Club admitted the Kuvasz to its Stud Book; in 1934 ten new dogs were registered. The breed began to gain acceptance. Around 1939 a Kuvasz Club was formed, and there is evidence of much breed activity at that time. Kuvaszok were frequently exhibited and several gained championship status. The Romanse Kennels became inactive in the 1940s after the death of Mr. Rowe. Mrs. Rowe died in 1956.

In 1946, Dickens Von Leonardshof was imported from Germany by Mr. and Mrs. Frank Zeigler of Manchester, Pennsylvania. She was paid for with food packages. Later bred to their 1947 import, Rike Von Waldfrid, she produced ten puppies. They were all exhibited at Morris and Essex, Madison Square Garden and other shows gaining championship for Rike, thus making her eligible for registration with the AKC. The Zieglers continued exhibiting for several years, but due to advanced age, they too became inactive in the 1950s.

Except for occasional litters and very occasional exhibition, the Kuvasz stayed comparatively inactive until 1966. In January 1966, the first issue of the *Kuvasz Newsletter* appeared, which helped to find Kuvasz owners and those interested in the breed, and led to the formation of the Kuvasz Club of America on April 30, 1966.

BREED REQUIREMENTS

HOUSING AND SHELTER

A sturdy, hardy fellow, the Kuvasz need not and should not be pampered. Apart from the great need for love and companionship his demands are modest. In his native land he is exposed to the most extreme climatic conditions. Sub-zero winters followed by hot

The Kuvasz's coat serves as an insulation against the cold as well as heat. Young puppies, however, should not be kept outside in the snow for too long. Owner, Karpati Kennels.

summers through the centuries adjusted him for survival under any geographic location.

It cannot be overemphasized that the Kuvasz is a working dog. He will prefer to stay outside most of the time. His coat serves as an insulation against cold as well as heat and therefore should never be cut. In the summer he needs a shaded area to protect him from heat and his coat from yellowing due to overexposure to sun. During cold winter months he needs a draft-free dry shelter just large enough to accommodate him comfortably. Heating of his winter outdoor housing is unnecessary for a mature dog. Very young dogs and whelping bitches naturally need more attention.

EXERCISE

The Kuvasz, like any other large breed, is not recommended for apartment living unless his owner is willing to devote considerable time to the dog's daily exercise. Due to his active nature and large size it is a basic need for this breed to get sufficient exercise, regardless of the type of home he lives in. It is advisable to walk the dog and to occasionally offer him the opportunity to run in open areas where he can really stretch his body and show off the beauty of his movement.

ADAPTABILITY TO TRAINING

The Kuvasz loves to work, however, he works best for his owners, for those he loves and respects. The mature dog does not favor corrections and orders

Due to his active nature and large size, the Kuvasz demands a good amount of exercise. Offer him the opportunity to run in open areas where he can stretch his limbs. Owner, Karpati Kennels.

Ch. Asgard LoFranco I Want It All, CD, TD, NA, owned by Deb Eldredge, became the first Agility-titled Kuvasz.

from strangers. His intelligence requires some training from an early age. Correct early training will lay the base for a good understanding between owner and dog and for more sophisticated training and commands in the future.

The excellent qualities of body structure and mental make-up make him a prime candidate for the highest degrees of obedience training, including high and long jumps. Jumping, however, should be attempted with professional guidance and at physical maturity of the dog as it might be harmful to the bone structure in the developing stage of a too-young animal.

Ch. Asgard LoFranco I Want It All, CD, TD, NA, owned by Deb Eldredge, became the third Kuvasz ever to earn a Tracking title and the first Champion to do so.

Ch. Asgard LoFranco I Want It All, CD, TD, NA, owned by Deb Eldredge, earned his CD in February 1996 to become the first triple-titled Kuvasz.

THE COAT AND ITS CARE

INTRODUCTION

The coat of the Kuvasz is always white, but there is considerable variation in its type. It is always medium coarse in texture but ranges from quite wavy to straight, yet is never too curly and should not have any tendency to mat or to cord. The distribution of the coat follows a definite pattern regardless of type. The head, muzzle, ears, front of forelegs and hind legs below the thighs are covered with short, smooth coat. The backs of front legs are feathered to the pasterns with medium length hair. The body and sides of the

The Kuvasz has a double coat that ranges from straight to quite wavy.

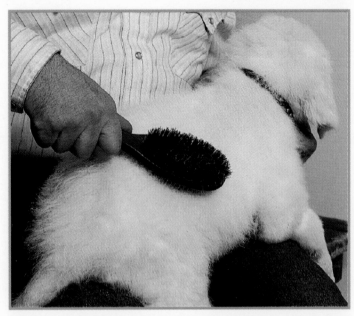

The Kuvasz should be brushed daily with a good quality rubber-cushioned pin brush followed by a light brushing with a boar bristle brush for the finishing touches. Owner, Karpati Kennels.

thighs are covered with heavy coat also of medium length. The longest coat is on the back of thighs and the tail where it reaches about six inches.

In different geographic locations and climatic conditions the density of the coat varies. In warm, summer months the Kuvasz loses his woolly undercoat and may lose some of his long outer coat. Full, luxuriant coat comes back by the early winter months.

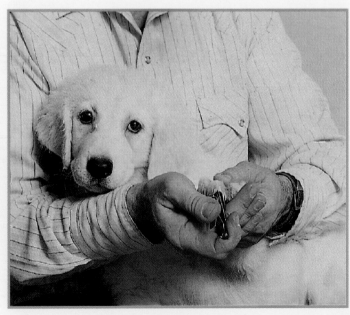

Begin trimming your Kuvasz's nails at an early age so that he will become used to the procedure. Be careful not to cut too close to the vein or quick. Owner, Karpati Kennels.

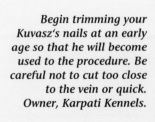

33

GROOMING

Looking at the pristine whiteness of this coat, one is apt to presume that the Kuvasz needs frequent bathing and expensive grooming. This is not so. The texture of his coat is such that it resists dirt. As a general rule, all dogs should be bathed as seldom as possible. Soaps and shampoos wash out the coat's natural oils, frequently causing skin irritation and dry lifeless coat. Just a few minutes of care per day is required to keep the Kuvasz in beautiful condition. The coat is brushed with a good quality rubber cushioned pin brush. Most dogs enjoy having their skin scratched, therefore the brushing may be done quite vigorously, taking care that the coat is not painfully pulled. The areas that need special attention are: behind the ears where the coat is extremely fine, on the back of thighs where it is long and very thick and on the tail. After making certain that there are not tangles, the pin brush grooming may be followed by the light brushing with a pure boar's bristle brush for a "finishing touch." Brushing is done in layers starting at the lower portions and holding up the excess hair with the free hand.

BATHING

The Kuvasz that is being exhibited may require a bath a few days before a show. It is not advisable to bathe the dog the day before, because bathing softens the coat, causes a loss of natural texture and may cause excessive shedding. There are some excellent shampoos on the market especially formulated for dogs and are preferable to human hair preparations for use in dog bathing. Hair preparations made for human use would be avoided as they are usually too harsh for dogs. On a warm summer day, it is all right to bathe the dog outdoors using the garden hose. He need not even be towel dried. He will shake most of the water off and dry in a short time. His owner would do well to walk him on the leash for sometime, preventing him from rolling in the grass.

In the wintertime, in very cold climates, wet baths should be completely avoided. The coat can be very successfully dry-cleaned by rubbing in it white powdered corn starch and then brushing it out thoroughly. If for some reason winter bathing cannot be avoided, it must done indoors in luke warm water. The coat should be first towel dried and finished with

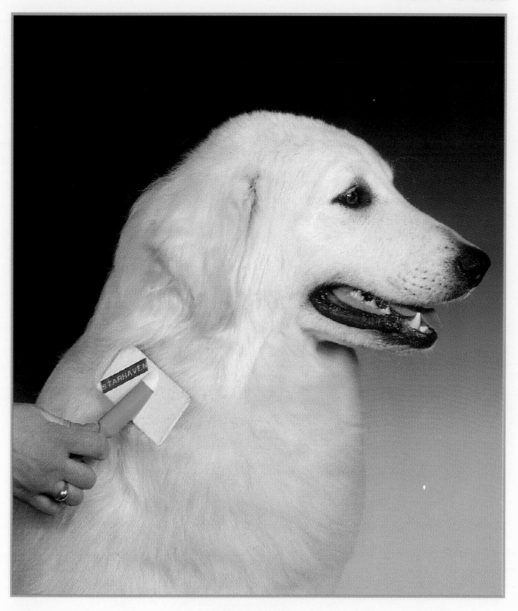

Most Kuvasz enjoy having their skin scratched, so they will love a vigorous brushing. Take care that the coat is not pulled too roughly. Owner, Joseph A. Zielinski.

a hand hair dryer. The dog must be kept indoors for several hours after his coat appears dry.

THE SHOW DOG

At dog shows, the Kuvasz should be presented in a completely natural but immaculately clean condition. Except for possible straggle hairs on the hocks and between the pads, his coat is never trimmed and his whiskers never cutoff. The long "eye-brows" occasionally curl into the dog's eyes and should be cut at about half point.

YOUR PUPPY'S NEW HOME

Before actually collecting your puppy, it is better that you purchase the basic items you will need in advance of the pup's arrival date. This allows you more opportunity to shop around and ensure you have exactly what you want rather than having to buy lesser quality in a hurry.

It is always better to collect the puppy as early in the day as possible. In most instances this will mean that the puppy has a few hours with your family before it is time to retire for his first night's sleep away from his former home.

If the breeder is local, then you may not need any form of box to place the puppy in when you bring him

Choosing the right Kuvasz puppy for you may be a difficult decision to make. Once you pick your puppy, be sure you are prepared for his arrival in your home. Owner, Karpati Kennels.

A reputable breeder will help to make your Kuvasz puppy's transition to his new home much easier for the puppy—and for you! Owner, Karpati Kennels.

home. A member of the family can hold the pup in his lap—duly protected by some towels just in case the puppy becomes car sick! Be sure to advise the breeder at what time you hope to arrive for the puppy, as this will obviously influence the feeding of the pup that morning or afternoon. If you arrive early in the day, then they will likely only give the pup a light breakfast so as to reduce the risk of travel sickness.

If the trip will be of a few hours duration, you should take a travel crate with you. The crate will provide your pup with a safe place to lie down and rest during the trip. During the trip, the puppy will no doubt wish to relieve his bowels, so you will have to make a few stops. On a long journey you may need a rest yourself, and can take the opportunity to let the puppy get some fresh air. However, do not let the puppy walk where there may have been a lot of other dogs because he might pick up an infection. Also, if he relieves his bowels at such a time, do not just leave the feces where they were dropped. This is the height of irresponsibility. It has resulted in many public parks and other places actually banning dogs. You can purchase poop-scoops from your pet shop and should have them with you whenever you are taking the dog out where he might foul a public place.

Your journey home should be made as quickly as possible. If it is a hot day, be sure the car interior is amply supplied with fresh air. It should never be too hot or too cold for the puppy. The pup must never be placed where he might be subject to a draft. If the journey requires an overnight stop at a motel, be

Once your Kuvasz puppy has received all of his vaccinations, he can begin to explore his yard. Before this time, a puppy is very susceptible to bacteria and disease. Owner, Deb Eldredge.

aware that other guests will not appreciate a puppy crying half the night. You must regard the puppy as a baby and comfort him so he does not cry for long periods. The worst thing you can do is to shout at or smack him. This will mean your relationship is off to a really bad start. You wouldn't smack a baby, and your puppy is still very much just this.

ON ARRIVING HOME

By the time you arrive home the puppy may be very tired, in which case he should be taken to his sleeping area and allowed to rest. Children should not be allowed to interfere with the pup when he is sleeping. If the pup is not tired, he can be allowed to investigate his new home—but always under your close supervision. After a short look around, the puppy will no doubt appreciate a light meal and a drink of water. Do not overfeed him at his first meal because he will be in an excited state and more likely to be sick.

Although it is an obvious temptation, you should not invite friends and neighbors around to see the new arrival until he has had at least 48 hours in which to settle down. Indeed, if you can delay this longer then do so, especially if the puppy is not fully vaccinated. At the very least, the visitors might introduce some local bacteria on their clothing that the puppy is not immune to. This aspect is always a risk when a pup has been moved some distance, so the fewer people the pup meets in the first week or so the better.

Puppies love to chew on things, so make sure that all electrical appliances are neatly hidden from view and unplugged when not in use.

DANGERS IN THE HOME

Your home holds many potential dangers for a little mischievous puppy, so you must think about these in advance and be sure he is protected from them. The more obvious are as follows:

Open Fires. All open fires should be protected by a mesh screen guard so there is no danger of the pup being burned by spitting pieces of coal or wood.

Electrical Wires. Puppies just love chewing on things, so be sure that all electrical appliances are neatly hidden from view and are not left plugged in when not in use. It is not sufficient simply to turn the plug switch to the off position—pull the plug from the socket.

Open Doors. A door would seem a pretty innocuous object, yet with a strong draft it could kill or injure a puppy easily if it is slammed shut. Always ensure there is no risk of this happening. It is most likely

A toy can be a potential danger for a small puppy. Make sure that any toys your puppy plays with are safe and do not have small parts that can be removed and swallowed.

Open doors can be dangerous to small puppies. At any time a gust of wind can blow through and slam a door shut, which could easily injure a puppy.

during warm weather when you have windows or outside doors open and a sudden gust of wind blows through.

Balconies. If you live in a high-rise building, obviously the pup must be protected from falling. Be sure he cannot get through any railings on your patio, balcony, or deck.

Ponds and Pools. A garden pond or a swimming pool is a very dangerous place for a little puppy to be near. Be sure it is well screened so there is no risk of the pup falling in. It takes barely a minute for a pup—or a child—to drown.

The Kitchen. While many puppies will be kept in the kitchen, at least while they are toddlers and not able to control their bowel movements, this is a room full of danger—especially while you are cooking. When cooking, keep the puppy in a play pen or in another room where he is safely out of harm's way. Alternatively, if you have a carry box or crate, put him in this so he can still see you but is well protected.

Be aware, when using washing machines, that more than one puppy has clambered in and decided to have a nap and received a wash instead! If you leave the washing machine door open and leave the room for any reason, then be sure to check inside the machine before you close the door and switch on.

Small Children. Toddlers and small children should never be left unsupervised with puppies. In spite of such advice it is amazing just how many people not only do this but also allow children to pull and maul pups. They should be taught from the outset that a puppy is not a plaything to be dragged about the home—and they should be promptly scolded if they disobey.

Children must be shown how to lift a puppy so it is safe. Failure by you to correctly educate your children about dogs could one day result in their getting a very nasty bite or scratch. When a puppy is lifted, his weight must always be supported. To lift the pup, first place your right hand under his chest. Next, secure the pup by using your left hand to hold his neck. Now you can lift him and bring him close to your chest. Never lift a pup by his ears and, while he can be lifted by the scruff of his neck where the fur is loose, there is no reason ever to do this, so don't.

Beyond the dangers already cited you may be able to think of other ones that are specific to your home—steep basement steps or the like. Go around your home and check out all potential problems—you'll be glad you did.

THE FIRST NIGHT

The first few nights a puppy spends away from his mother and littermates are quite traumatic for him. He will feel very lonely, maybe cold, and will certainly miss the heartbeat of his siblings when sleeping. To help overcome his loneliness it may help to place a clock next to his bed—one with a loud tick. This will in some way soothe him, as the clock ticks to a rhythm not dissimilar from a heart beat. A cuddly toy may also help in the first few weeks. A dim nightlight may provide some comfort to the puppy, because his eyes will not yet be fully able to see in the dark. The puppy may want to leave his bed for a drink or to relieve himself.

If the pup does whimper in the night, there are two things you should not do. One is to get up and chastise him, because he will not understand why you are shouting at him; and the other is to rush to comfort him every time he cries because he will quickly realize that if he wants you to come running all he needs to do is to holler loud enough!

By all means give your puppy some extra attention on his first night, but after this quickly refrain from so doing. The pup will cry for a while but then settle down and go to sleep. Some pups are, of course, worse than others in this respect, so you must use balanced judgment in the matter. Many owners take their pups to bed with them, and there is certainly nothing wrong with this.

The pup will be no trouble in such cases. However, you should only do this if you intend to let this be a

Kuvasz puppies will get along just fine with other pets as long as the introduction is made under careful supervision. Stormy is Winter's favorite friend and playmate.

permanent arrangement, otherwise it is hardly fair to the puppy. If you have decided to have two puppies, then they will keep each other company and you will have few problems.

OTHER PETS

If you have other pets in the home then the puppy must be introduced to them under careful supervision. Puppies will get on just fine with any other pets— but you must make due allowance for the respective sizes of the pets concerned, and appreciate that your puppy has a rather playful nature. It would be very foolish to leave him with a young rabbit. The pup will want to play and might bite the bunny and get altogether too rough with it. Kittens are more able to defend themselves from overly cheeky pups, who will get a quick scratch if they overstep the mark. The adult cat could obviously give the pup a very bad scratch, though generally cats will jump clear of pups and watch them from a suitable vantage point. Eventually they will meet at ground level where the cat will quickly hiss and box a puppy's ears. The pup will soon learn to respect an adult cat; thereafter they will probably develop into great friends as the pup matures into an adult dog.

HOUSETRAINING

Undoubtedly, the first form of training your puppy will undergo is in respect of his toilet habits. To achieve this you can use either newspaper, or a large litter tray filled with soil or lined with newspaper. A

Housebreaking should begin when the pup is still with his breeders. Once you bring your new puppy home, use the same type of material the puppy is used to eliminating on during the first stages of housebreaking.

puppy cannot control his bowels until he is a few months old, and not fully until he is an adult. Therefore you must anticipate his needs and be prepared for a few accidents. The prime times a pup will urinate and defecate are shortly after he wakes up from a sleep, shortly after he has eaten, and after he has been playing awhile. He will usually whimper and start searching the room for a suitable place. You must quickly pick him up and place him on the newspaper or in the litter tray. Hold him in position gently but firmly. He might jump out of the box without doing anything on the first one or two occasions, but if you simply repeat the procedure every time you think he wants to relieve himself then eventually he will get the message.

When he does defecate as required, give him plenty of praise, telling him what a good puppy he is. The litter tray or newspaper must, of course, be cleaned or replaced after each use—puppies do not like using a dirty toilet any more than you do. The pup's toilet can be placed near the kitchen door and as he gets older the tray can be placed outside while the door is open. The pup will then start to use it while he is outside. From that time on, it is easy to get the pup to use a given area of the yard. Feces should be trashed or dug into the soil so they create no health risk.

It is not difficult to train the pup, once he is a little older, to use a given area of your yard as his toilet. This is preferable to him fouling flower beds or pathways. Remember though, he will only be clean in his habits if you teach him to be. Toilet training should never be a problem if you proceed as suggested. When dogs become dirty in their own home, it is invariably because their owner was not consistent when the dog was a pup, and so the dog was never correctly housetrained. Training should never require any form of punishment for it is a wholly natural act and requires only your guidance and patience.

THE EARLY DAYS

You will no doubt be given much advice on how to bring up your puppy. This will come from dog-owning friends, neighbors, and through articles and books you may read on the subject. Some of the advice will be sound, some will be nothing short of rubbish. What you should do above all else is to keep an open mind and let common sense prevail over prejudice and worn-out ideas that have been handed down over the centuries. There is no one way that is superior to all others, no more than there is no one dog that is exactly a replica of another. Each is an individual and must always be regarded as such.

A dog never becomes disobedient, unruly, or a menace to society without the full consent of his owner. Your puppy may have many limitations, but the singular biggest limitation he is confronted with in so many instances is his owner's inability to understand his needs and how to cope with them.

IDENTIFICATION

It is a sad reflection on our society that the number of dogs and cats stolen every year runs into many thousands. To these can be added the number that get lost. If you do not want your cherished pet to be lost or stolen, then you should see that he is carrying a permanent identification number, as well as a temporary tag on his collar.

Permanent markings come in the form of tattoos placed either inside the pup's ear flap, or on the inner side of a pup's upper rear leg. The number given is then recorded with one of the national registration companies. Research laboratories will not purchase dogs carrying numbers as they realize these are clearly someone's pet, and not abandoned animals. As a result, thieves will normally abandon dogs so marked and this at least gives the dog a chance to be taken to the police or the dog pound, when the number can be traced and the dog reunited with its family. The only problem with this method at this time is that there are a number of registration bodies, so it is not always apparent which one the dog is registered with (as you provide the actual number). However, each registration body is aware of his competitors and will normally be happy to supply their addresses. Those holding the dog can check out which one you are with. It is not a perfect system, but until such is developed it's the best available.

A temporary tag takes the form of a metal or plastic disk large enough for you to place the dog's name and your phone number on it—maybe even your address as well. In virtually all places you will be required to obtain a license for your puppy. This may not become applicable until the pup is six months old, but it might

Your new Kuvasz puppy will depend on you for everything; it is up to you as his new owner to fully understand his needs and how to cope with them.

apply regardless of his age. Much depends upon the state within a country, or the country itself, so check with your veterinarian if the breeder has not already advised you on this.

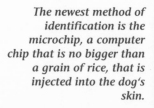

The newest method of identification is the microchip, a computer chip that is no bigger than a grain of rice, that is injected into the dog's skin.

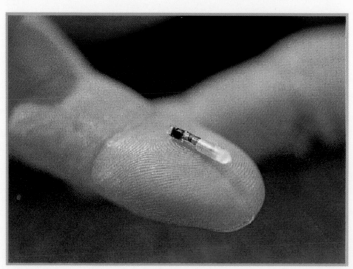

FEEDING YOUR PUPPY OR DOG

Dog owners today are fortunate in that they live in an age when considerable cash has been invested in the study of canine nutritional requirements. This means dog food manufacturers are very concerned about ensuring that their foods are of the best quality. The result of all of their studies, apart from the food itself, is that dog owners are bombarded with advertisements telling them why they must purchase a given brand. The number of products available to you is unlimited, so it is hardly surprising to find that dogs in general suffer from obesity and an excess of vitamins, rather than the reverse. The nutrition of your dog must take account of many factors, which is why no company can tell you exactly how much you should feed your puppy. At best, they can offer only guidelines, and even these may be far from accurate.

FACTORS AFFECTING NUTRITIONAL NEEDS

Activity Level. A dog that lives in a country environment and is able to exercise for long periods of the day will need more food than the same breed of dog living in an apartment and given little exercise.

Quality of the Food. Obviously the quality of food will affect the quantity required by a puppy. If the nutritional content of a food is low then the puppy will need more of it than if a better quality food was fed.

Balance of Nutrients and Vitamins. Feeding a puppy the correct balance of nutrients is not easy because the average person is not able to measure out ratios of one to another, so it is a case of trying to see that nothing is in excess. However, only tests, or your veterinarian, can be the source of reliable advice.

Genetic and Biological Variation. Apart from all of the other considerations, it should be remembered that each puppy is an individual. His genetic make-up will influence not only his physical characteristics but also his metabolic efficiency. This being so, two pups from the same litter can vary quite a bit in the amount of food they need to perform the same function under the same conditions. If you consider the potential combinations of all of these factors then you will see that pups of a given breed could vary quite a bit in the amount of food they will need. Before discussing feeding quantities it is valuable to know at least a little about the composition of food and its role in the body.

POPpups™ are 100% edible and enhanced with dog-friendly ingredients like liver, cheese, spinach, chicken, carrots, or potatoes. They contain no salt, sugar, alcohol, plastic or preservatives. You can even microwave a POPpup™ to turn into a huge crackly treat.

COMPOSITION AND ROLE OF FOOD

The main ingredients of food are protein, fats, and carbohydrates, each of which is needed in

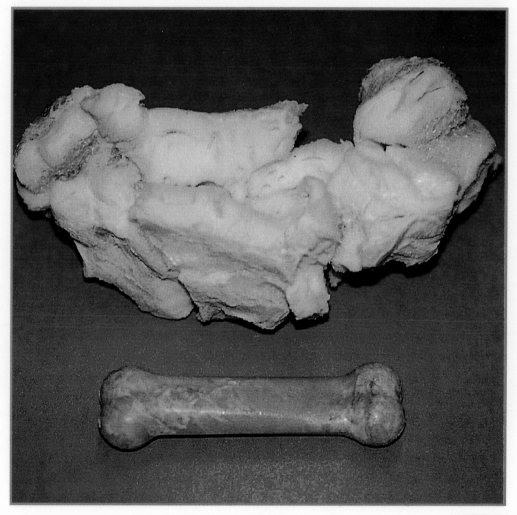

relatively large quantities when compared to the other needs of vitamins and minerals. The other vital ingredient of food is, of course, water. Although all foods obviously contain some of the basic ingredients needed for an animal to survive, they do not all contain the ingredients in the needed ratios or type. For example, there are many forms of protein, just as there are many types of carbohydrates. Both of these compounds are found in meat and in vegetable matter—but not all of those that are needed will be in one particular meat or vegetable. Plants, especially, do not contain certain amino acids that are required for the synthesis of certain proteins needed by dogs.

Likewise, vitamins are found in meats and vegetable matter, but vegetables are a richer source of most. Meat contains very little carbohydrates. Some vitamins can be synthesized by the dog, so do not need to be supplied via the food. Dogs are carnivores and this means their digestive tract has evolved to need a high quantity of meat as compared to humans. The digestive system of carnivores is unable to break down the tough cellulose walls of plant matter, but it is easily able to assimilate proteins from meat.

In order to gain its needed vegetable matter in a form that it can cope with, the carnivore eats all of its prey. This includes the partly digested food within the stomach. In commercially prepared foods, the cellulose is broken down by cooking. During this process the vitamin content is either greatly reduced or lost altogether. The manufacturer therefore adds vitamins once the heat process has been completed. This is why commercial foods are so useful as part of a feeding regimen, providing they are of good quality and from a company that has prepared the foods very carefully.

Opposite: When you bring your puppy home, continue to feed the same brand the breeder was feeding. If you are going to change the brand of food, do so gradually. Owner, Karpati Kennels.

Proteins

These are made from amino acids, of which at least ten are essential if a puppy is to maintain healthy growth. Proteins provide the building blocks for the puppy's body. The richest sources are meat, fish and poultry, together with their by-products. The latter will include milk, cheese, yogurt, fishmeal, and eggs. Vegetable matter that has a high protein content includes soy beans, together with numerous corn and other plant extracts that have been

dehydrated. The actual protein content needed in the diet will be determined both by the activity level of the dog and his age. The total protein need will also be influenced by the digestibility factor of the food given.

Fats

These serve numerous roles in the puppy's body. They provide insulation against the cold, and help buffer the organs from knocks and general activity shocks. They provide the richest source of energy, and reserves of this, and they are vital in the transport of vitamins and other nutrients, via the blood, to all other organs. Finally, it is the fat content within a diet that gives it palatability. It is important that the fat content of a diet should not be excessive. This is because the high energy content of fats (more than twice that of protein or carbohydrate) will increase the overall energy content of the diet. The puppy will adjust its food intake to that of its energy needs, which are obviously more easily met in a high-energy diet. This will mean that while the fats are providing the energy needs of the puppy, the overall diet may not be providing its protein, vitamin, and mineral needs, so signs of protein deficiency will become apparent. Rich sources of fats are meat, their byproducts (butter, milk), and vegetable oils, such as safflower, olive, corn or soy bean.

Carrots are rich in fiber, carbohydrates, and vitamin A. The Carrot Bone™ by Nylabone® is a durable chew containing no plastics or artificial ingredients and it can be served as-is, in a bone-hard form, or microwaved to a biscuit consistency.

Carbohydrates

These are the principal energy compounds given to puppies and adult dogs. Their inclusion within most commercial brand dog foods is for cost, rather than dietary needs. These compounds are more commonly known as sugars, and they are seen in simple or complex compounds of carbon, hydrogen, and oxygen. One of the simple sugars is called glucose, and it is vital to many metabolic processes. When large chains of glucose are created, they form compound sugars. One of these is called glycogen, and it is found in the cells of animals. Another, called starch, is the material that is found in the cells of plants.

Vitamins

These are not foods as such but chemical compounds that assist in all aspects of an animal's life. They help in so many ways that to attempt to describe these effectively would require a chapter in itself. Fruits are a rich source of vitamins, as is the liver of most animals. Many vitamins are unstable and easily destroyed by light, heat, moisture, or rancidity. An excess of vitamins, especially A and D, has been proven to be very harmful. Provided a puppy is receiving a balanced diet, it is most unlikely there will be a deficiency, whereas hypervitaminosis (an excess of vitamins) has become quite common due to owners and breeders feeding unneeded supplements. The only time you should feed extra vitamins to your puppy is if your veterinarian advises you to.

Minerals

These provide strength to bone and cell tissue, as well as assist in many metabolic processes. Examples are calcium, phosphorous, copper, iron, magnesium, selenium, potassium, zinc, and sodium. The recommended amounts of all minerals in the diet has not been fully established. Calcium and phosphorous are known to be important, especially to puppies. They help in forming strong bone. As with vitamins, a mineral deficiency is most unlikely in pups given a good and varied diet. Again, an excess can create problems—this applying equally to calcium.

Water

This is the most important of all nutrients, as is easily shown by the fact that the adult dog is made up of about 60 percent water, the puppy containing

an even higher percentage. Dogs must retain a water balance, which means that the total intake should be balanced by the total output. The intake comes either by direct input (the tap or its equivalent), plus water released when food is oxidized, known as metabolic water (remember that all foods contain the elements hydrogen and oxygen that recombine in the body to create water). A dog without adequate water will lose condition more rapidly than one depleted of food, a fact common to most animal species.

Water is the most important of all nutrients. Make sure that your Kuvasz has access to fresh clean water at all times. Owner, Linda Lloyd.

AMOUNT TO FEED

I am always rather uneasy when asked how much I would recommend feeding a puppy or dog. This is because many factors will determine the individual's needs. The best way to determine dietary requirements is by observing the puppy's general health and physical appearance. If he is well covered with flesh, shows good bone development and muscle, and is an active alert puppy, then his diet is fine. A puppy will consume about twice as much as an adult (of the same breed). You should ask the breeder of your puppy to show you the amounts fed to their pups and this will be a good starting point.

The puppy should eat his meal in about five to seven minutes. Any leftover food can be discarded or placed into the refrigerator until the next meal (but be sure it is thawed fully if your fridge is very cold).

If the puppy quickly devours its meal and is clearly still hungry, then you are not giving him enough food. If he eats readily but then begins to pick at it, or walks away leaving a quantity, then you are probably giving him too much food. Adjust this at the next meal and you will quickly begin to appreciate what the correct amount is. If, over a number of weeks, the pup starts to look fat, then he is obviously overeating; the reverse is true if he starts to look thin compared with others of the same breed.

WHEN TO FEED

It really does not matter what times of the day the puppy is fed, as long as he receives the needed quantity of food. Puppies from 8 weeks to 12 or 16 weeks need 3 or 4 meals a day. Older puppies and adult dogs should be fed twice a day. What is most important is that the feeding times are reasonably regular. They can be tailored to fit in with your own timetable—for example, 7 a.m. and 6 p.m. The dog will then expect his meals at these times each day. Keeping regular feeding times and feeding set amounts will help you monitor your puppy's or dog's health. If a dog that's normally enthusiastic about mealtimes and eats readily suddenly shows a lack of interest in food, you'll know something's not right.

TRAINING YOUR CANINE FAMILY MEMBER

Once your puppy has settled into your home and responds to his name, then you can begin his basic training. Before giving advice on how you should go about doing this, two important points should be made. You should train the puppy in isolation of any potential distractions, and you should keep all lessons very short. It is essential that you have the full attention of your puppy. This is not possible if there are other people about, or televisions and radios on, or other pets in the vicinity. Even when the pup has become a young adult, the maximum time you should allocate to a lesson is about 20 minutes. However, you can give the puppy more than one lesson a day, three being as many as are recommended, each well spaced apart.

Before beginning a lesson, always play a little game with the puppy so he is in an active state of mind and thus more receptive to the matter at hand. Likewise, always end a lesson with fun-time for the pup, and always—this is most important—end on a high note, praising the puppy. Let the lesson end when the pup has done as you require so he receives lots of fuss. This will really build his confidence.

COLLAR AND LEASH TRAINING

Training a puppy to his collar and leash is very easy. Place a collar on the puppy and, although he will initially try to bite at it, he will soon forget it, the more so if you play with him. You can leave the collar on for a few hours. Some people leave their dogs' collars on all of the time, others only when they are taking the dog out. If it is to be left on, purchase a narrow or round one so it does not mark the fur.

Once the puppy ignores his collar, then you can attach the leash to it and let the puppy pull this along behind it for a few minutes. However, if the pup starts to chew at the leash, simply hold the leash but keep it slack and let the pup go where he wants. The idea is to let him get the feel of the leash, but not get in the habit of chewing it. Repeat this a couple of times a day for two days and the pup will get used to the leash without thinking that it will restrain him—which you will not have attempted to do yet.

Next, you can let the pup understand that the leash will restrict his movements. The first time he realizes this, he will pull and buck or just sit down. Immediately call the pup to you and give him lots of fuss. Never tug on the leash so the puppy is dragged along the floor, as this simply implants a negative thought in his mind. All of this leash training can be done in the home or in the yard. After a few lessons, the puppy will be familiar with the restriction on the leash and you can then increase this by going in a direction opposite to the pup. Give the leash a short tug so the pup is brought to a halt and call the pup to you enthusiastically, then continue walking. When the puppy is walking happily on the leash, then it is time to end the lesson with lots of praise. There is no rush over leash training, so let

Training your Kuvasz puppy to a collar is very easy. Place the collar on the puppy and, although he will try to bite it at first, he will soon forget that he is even wearing it.

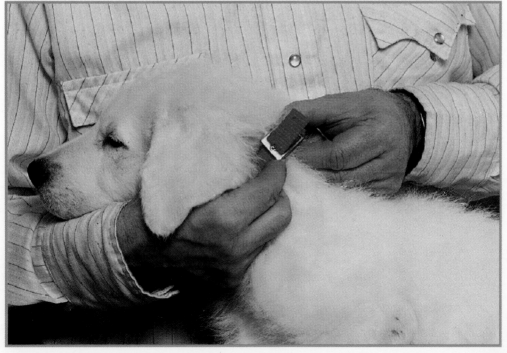

it take quite a few days if need be. You want to coax the puppy to go in the direction you want after he has sniffed around and gone the way he chose initially.

THE SIT COMMAND

As with most basic commands, your puppy will learn this one in just a few lessons. You can give the puppy two lessons a day on the sit command but he will make just as much progress with one 15-minute lesson each day. Some trainers will advise you that you should not proceed to other commands until the previous one has been learned really well. However, a bright young pup is quite capable of handling more than one command per lesson, and certainly per day. Indeed, as time progresses, you will be going through each command as a matter of routine before a new one is attempted. This is so the puppy always starts, as well as ends, a lesson on a high note, having successfully completed something.

Call the puppy to you and fuss over him. Place one hand on his hindquarters and the other under his upper chest. Say "Sit" in a pleasant (never harsh)

Bubba and owner Tom Eldredge are successful in Pee Wee Handling. Here they demonstrate the sit command.

voice. At the same time, push down his rear end and push up under his chest. The pup will be forced to sit. Now lavish praise on the puppy. Repeat this a few times and your pet will get the idea. Once the puppy is in the sit position you will release your hands. At first he will tend to get up, so immediately repeat the exercise. The lesson will end when the pup is in the sit position. When the puppy understands the command, and does it right away, you can slowly move backwards so that you are a few feet away from him. If he attempts to come to you, simply place him back in the original position and start again. Do not attempt to keep the pup in the sit position for too long. At this age, even a few seconds is a long while and you do not want him to get bored with lessons before he has even begun them.

THE HEEL COMMAND

All dogs should be able to walk nicely on a leash without their owners being involved in a tug-of-war. The heel command will follow leash training. Heel training is best done where you have a wall to one side of you. This will restrict the puppy's lateral movements, so you only have to contend with forward and backward situations. A fence is an alternative, or you can do the lesson in the garage. Again, it is better to do the lesson in private, not on a public sidewalk where there will be many distractions.

With a puppy, there will be no need to use a choke collar as you can be just as effective with a regular one. The leash should be of good length, certainly not too short. You can adjust the space between you, the puppy, and the wall so your pet has only a small amount of room to move sideways. This being so, he will either hang back or pull ahead—the latter is the more desirable state as it indicates a bold pup who is not frightened of you.

Hold the leash in your right hand and pass it through your left. As the puppy moves ahead and strains on the leash, give the leash a quick jerk backwards with your left hand, at the same time saying "Heel." The position you want the pup to be in is such that his chest is level with, or just behind, an imaginary line from your knee. When the puppy is in this position, praise him and begin walking again, and the whole exercise will be repeated. Once the puppy begins to get the message, you can use your left hand to pat the side of your knee so the pup is encouraged to keep close to your side.

It is useful to suddenly do an about-turn when the pup understands the basics. This will result in a sudden jerk as you move in the opposite direction. The puppy will now be behind you, so you can pat your knee and say "Heel." As soon as the pup is in the correct position, give him lots of praise. The puppy will now be beginning to associate certain words with certain actions. Whenever he is not in the heel position he will experience displeasure as you jerk the leash, but when he comes alongside you he will receive praise. Given these two options, he will always prefer the latter—assuming he has no other reason to fear you, which would then create a dilemma in his mind.

Once the lesson has been well learned, then you can adjust your pace from a slow walk to a quick one and the puppy will come to adjust. The slow walk is always the more difficult for most puppies, as they are usually anxious to be on the move.

If you have no wall to walk against then things will be a little more difficult because the pup will tend to wander to his left. This means you need to give lateral jerks as well as bring the pup to your side. End the lesson when the pup is walking nicely beside you. Begin the lesson with a few sit commands (which he understands by now), so you're starting with success and praise. If your puppy is nervous on the leash, you should never drag him to your side as you may see so many other people do (who obviously didn't invest in a good book like you did!). If the pup sits down, call him to your side and give lots of praise. The pup must always come to you because he wants to. If he is dragged to your side he will see you doing the dragging—a big negative. When he races ahead he does not see you jerk the leash, so all he knows is that something restricted his movement and, once he was in a given position, you gave him lots of praise. This is using canine psychology to your advantage.

Always try to remember that if a dog must be disciplined, then try not to let him associate the discipline with you. This is not possible in all matters but, where it is, this is definitely to be preferred.

HEEL AND SIT

This is a direct follow on to the first two commands. It will hardly need instruction if both parts have been learned well. As you come to a halt in the heel position, tell the puppy to sit. If he fails to do this then simply lean over and press his hindquarters down, repeating the command. If the exercise is done a number of times then the pup will automatically sit when you come to a halt. It is useful when you stop to talk to a friend, or are waiting for traffic to clear before crossing a road.

THE STAY COMMAND

This command follows from the sit. Face the puppy and say "Sit." Now step backwards, and as you do, say "Stay." Let the pup remain in the position for only

Teaching the heel command will ensure that your Kuvasz will walk nicely beside you on a leash without pulling ahead or lagging behind. Owner, Deb Eldredge.

a few seconds before calling him to you and giving lots of praise. Repeat this, but step further back. You do not need to shout at the puppy. Your pet is not deaf; in fact, his hearing is far better than yours. Speak just loudly enough for the pup to hear, yet use a firm voice.

61

You can stretch the word to form a "sta-a-a-y." If the pup gets up and comes to you simply lift him up, place him back in the original position, and start again. As the pup comes to understand the command, you can move further and further back.

The next test is to walk away after placing the pup. This will mean your back is to him, which will tempt him to follow you. Keep an eye over your shoulder, and the minute the pup starts to move, spin around and, using a sterner voice, say either "Sit" or "Stay." If the pup has gotten quite close to you, then, again, return him to the original position.

As the weeks go by you can increase the length of time the pup is left in the stay position—but two to three minutes is quite long enough for a puppy. If your puppy drops into a lying position and is clearly more comfortable, there is nothing wrong with this. Likewise, your pup will want to face the direction in which you walked off. Some trainers will insist that the dog faces the direction he was placed in, regardless of whether you move off on his blind side. I have never believed in this sort of obedience because it has no practical benefit.

THE DOWN COMMAND

From the puppy's viewpoint, the down command can be one of the more difficult ones to accept. This is because the position is one taken up by a submissive dog in a wild pack situation. A timid dog will roll over—a natural gesture of submission. A bolder pup will want to get up, and might back off, not feeling he should have to submit to this command. He will feel that he is under attack from you and about to be punished—which is what would be the position in his natural environment. Once he comes to understand this is not the case, he will accept this unnatural position without any problem.

You may notice that some dogs will sit very quickly, but will respond to the down command more slowly— it is their way of saying that they will obey the command, but under protest!

There two ways to teach this command. One is, in my mind, more intimidating than the other, but it is up to you to decide which one works best for you. The first method is to stand in front of your puppy and bring him to the sit position, with his collar and leash on. Pass the leash under your left foot so that when you pull on it, the result is that the pup's neck is forced

Opposite: A well-mannered Kuvasz is a pleasure to own. Once your dog is fully trained, he will be ready to accompany you almost anywhere. Owner, Karpati Kennels.

downwards. With your free left hand, push the pup's shoulders down while at the same time saying "Down." This is when a bold pup will instantly try to back off and wriggle in full protest. Hold the pup firmly by the shoulders so he stays in the position for a second or two, then tell him what a good dog he is and give him lots of praise. Repeat this only a few times in a lesson because otherwise the puppy will get bored and upset over this command. End with an easy command that brings back the pup's confidence.

The second method, and the one I prefer, is done as follows: Stand in front of the pup and then tell him to sit. Now kneel down, which is immediately far less intimidating to the puppy than to have you towering above him. Take each of his front legs and pull them forward, at the same time saying "Down." Release the legs and quickly apply light pressure on the shoulders with your left hand. Then, as quickly, say "Good boy" and give lots of fuss. Repeat two or three times only. The pup will learn over a few lessons. Remember, this is a very submissive act on the pup's behalf, so there is no need to rush matters.

THE DOWN COMMAND

Once the puppy understands what is wanted, you can stand up and give the stay command. From the down command you can practice the down and stay, and then the sit and down—and down and sit. You should be able to move from one command to the other with no problem. If a problem is encountered, it is because the puppy has not understood a command or because you are making the lessons too long and boring with not enough praise in between commands. Some trainers will use food treats as rewards for each command learned, but this is not necessary. The puppy will do his exercises simply because they are part of his life and of being with you. It should not need bribes—your affection and praise are reward enough. If the puppy is obviously having an off day then do a simple exercise he knows well and then call it a day and play a game with him. Even dogs have their off days.

RECALL TO HEEL COMMAND

When your puppy is coming to the heel position from an off-leash situation—such as if he has been running free—he should do this in the correct manner. He should pass behind you and take up his position and then sit. To teach this command, have the pup in front of you in the sit position with his collar and leash on. Hold the leash in your right hand. Give him the command to heel, and pat your left knee. As the pup starts to move forward, use your right hand to guide him behind you. If need be you can hold his collar and walk the dog around the back of you to the desired position. You will need to repeat this a few times until the dog understands what is wanted.

When he has done this a number of times, you can try it without the collar and leash. If the pup comes up toward your left side, then bring him to the sit position in front of you, hold his collar and walk him around the back of you. He will eventually understand and automatically pass around your back each time. If the dog is already behind you when you recall him, then he should automatically come to your left side, which you will be patting with your hand.

THE NO COMMAND

This is a command that must be obeyed every time without fail. There are no halfway stages, he must be 100-percent reliable. Most delinquent dogs have never been taught this command; included in these are the jumpers, the barkers, and the biters. Were your puppy to approach a poisonous snake or any other potential danger, the no command, coupled with the recall, could save his life. You do not need to give a specific lesson for this command because it will crop up time and again in day-to-day life.

If the puppy is chewing a slipper, you should approach the pup, take hold of the slipper, and say "No" in a stern voice. If he jumps onto the furniture, lift him off and say "No" and place him gently on the floor. You must be consistent in the use of the command and apply it every time he is doing something you do not want him to do.

The commands discussed in this chapter are those that every puppy, regardless of his size or breed, should understand and obey without exception. You will note that in no instance is punishment used beyond a quick jerk on the leash or a gentle slap across his flanks. The emphasis is always on lavish praise when a task has been achieved.

YOUR HEALTHY DOG

Dogs, like all other animals, are capable of contracting problems and diseases that, in most cases, are easily avoided by sound husbandry—meaning well-bred and well-cared-for animals are less prone to developing diseases and problems than are carelessly bred and neglected animals. Your knowledge of how to avoid problems is far more valuable than all of the books and advice on how to cure them. Respectively, the only person you should listen to about treatment is your vet. Veterinarians don't have all the answers, but at least they are trained to analyze and treat illnesses, and are aware of the full implications of treatments. This does not mean a few old remedies aren't good standbys when all else fails, but in most cases modern science provides the best treatments for disease.

Opposite: Veterinarians are trained to analyze and treat illnesses. Having complete trust in your chosen veterinarian is tantamount to the long life of your dog.

PREVENTIVE PHILOSOPHY

If you are aware of how your puppy contracts a problem, you are more able to ensure that the chances of this happening are minimal. To become ill, certain conditions must be fulfilled. If they are not, your puppy's own defense system can cope with most problems that come his way (in small doses). Indeed, it is important that pups are in fact exposed to pathogens so they can build resistance to them. This does not mean you should purposely expose the pup to them.

Pathogenic organisms (bacterium and viruses) are all around you and your puppy. They are in the air, in the water, on your food (even when it is fresh and clean), and on your clothing and your household possessions. It is only when they reach infestation proportions that they are able to get a foothold and become parasitic enough to cause serious problems. To grow to unmanageable proportions they must live

in an environment conducive to such growth. This is an environment where there is little fresh air, where it is not too cold, and where there are no organisms—or chemicals—that can interrupt their reproductive progress.

They must then gain access to their victim—your puppy or dog—either via the food, via an intermediate host, via a wound, or by direct transfer. Having reached the puppy, it is still necessary for these pathogens to remain undetected for long enough to firmly establish themselves. If these conditions are met, pathogens begin to overcome the puppy's resistance and illness follows. This will happen in basically two ways. The parasites will colonize the surface of the dog, that is

A good veterinary facility will maintain a high standard of hygiene.

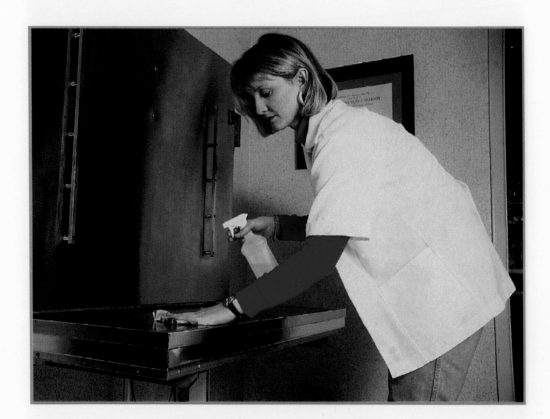

the skin, eyes, mouth, feet and so on, or they will enter its internal organs and migrate to those areas that are best suited to their parasitic mode of life. Because many internal disorders will exhibit the same clinical signs, they are far more of a problem to deal with than are external situations.

The major problem with internal disease and conditions is that you are often unaware that there is a problem until it is quite well advanced. Sometimes the problem cannot be determined until after the pup has died. Diagnosis is therefore crucial to internal disorders, and only a veterinarian is qualified, or able, to make such a diagnosis. This invariably requires microscopy, an understanding of staining techniques, and a knowledge of chemical and biological treatments.

CLEANLINESS IS HEALTHINESS

Your yard is an obvious source of potential problems, and an area in which your puppy will no doubt spend much time. Any feces left around will attract flies, which are one of the most common means of transferring bacteria from one place to another. A pile of rotting grass clippings is another potential hazard for your pup. Keep the yard tidy and remove any objects on which the puppy could cut himself. It only takes a minor lesion to allow pathogens to gain access to the puppy's internal system.

One very common way in which bacteria are transferred is via the owner's clothes or hands. For this reason some kennels will not allow visitors to touch the pups at all, and may well take even more stringent methods. Many establishments keep their pups behind glass doors in kennels simply to prevent visitors from handling them. If you should have reason to stroke, handle or otherwise come into contact with any dogs, cats or other pets not in your household, then be sure to wash your hands before you touch your puppy. Every precaution you take, as unimportant as it might seem, or as tedious, might be the very one that saves your puppy from a parasitic attack.

PHYSICAL EXAMS

Your puppy should receive regular physical examinations or check-ups. These come in two forms. One is obviously performed by your vet, and the other is a day-to-day procedure that should be done by you. Apart from the fact the exam will highlight any problem at an early stage, it is an excellent way of socializing the pup to being handled.

To do the physical exam yourself, start at the head and work your way around the body. You are looking for any sign of lesions, or any indication of parasites on the pup. The most common parasites are fleas and ticks.

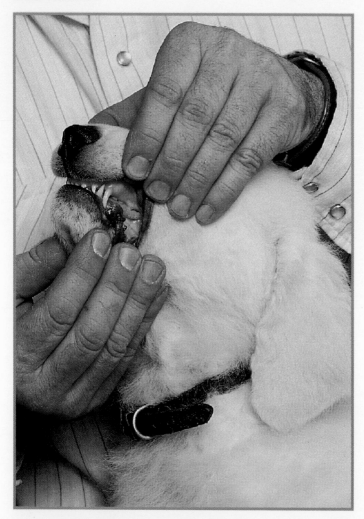

As your Kuvasz puppy's adult teeth begin to emerge, it is painful and annoying to him, and you must provide something safe for him to chew.

HEALTHY TEETH AND GUMS

Chewing is instinctual. Puppies chew so that their teeth and jaws grow strong and healthy as they develop. As the permanent teeth begin to emerge, it is painful and annoying to the puppy, and puppy owners must recognize that their new charges need something safe upon which to chew. Unfortunately, once the puppy's permanent teeth have emerged and settled solidly into the jaw, the chewing instinct does not fade. Adult dogs instinctively need to clean their teeth, massage their gums, and exercise their jaws through chewing.

It is necessary for your dog to have clean teeth. You should take your dog to the veterinarian at least once a year to have his teeth cleaned and to have his mouth examined for any sign of oral disease. Although dogs

The Hercules® by Nylabone® has raised dental tips that help fight plaque on your Kuvasz's teeth and gums.

do not get cavities in the same way humans do, dogs' teeth accumulate tartar, and more quickly than humans do! Veterinarians recommend brushing your dog's teeth daily. But who can find time to brush their dog's teeth daily? The accumulation of tartar and plaque on our dog's teeth when not removed can cause irritation and eventually erode the enamel and finally destroy the teeth. Advanced cases, while destroying the teeth, bring on gingivitis and periodontitis, two very serious conditions that can affect the dog's internal organs as well...to say nothing about bad breath!

Nylafloss® does wonders for your Kuvasz's dental health by massaging his gums and literally flossing between his teeth, loosening plaque and tartar build-up. Unlike cotton tug toys, Nylafloss® won't rot or fray.

Since everyone can't brush their dog's teeth daily or get to the veterinarian often enough for him to scale the dog's teeth, providing the dog with something safe to chew on will help maintain oral hygeine. Chew devices from Nylabone® keep dogs' teeth clean, but they also provide an excellent resource for entertainment and relief of doggie tensions. Nylabone® products give your dog something to do for an hour or two every day and during that hour or two, your dog will be taking an active part in keeping his teeth and gums healthy…without even realizing it! That's invaluable to your dog, and valuable to you!

Nylabone® provides fun bones, challenging bones, and *safe* bones. It is an owner's responsibility to recognize safe chew toys from dangerous ones. Your dog will chew and devour anything you give him. Dogs must not be permitted to chew on items that they can break. Pieces of broken objects can do internal damage to a dog, besides ripping the dog's mouth. Cheap plastic or rubber toys can cause stoppage in the intestines; such stoppages are operable only if caught immediately.

The most obvious choices, in this case, may be the worst choice. Natural beef bones were not designed for chewing and cannot take too much pressure from

Nylabone® is the only plastic dog bone made of 100% virgin nylon, specially processed to create a tough, durable, completely safe bone.

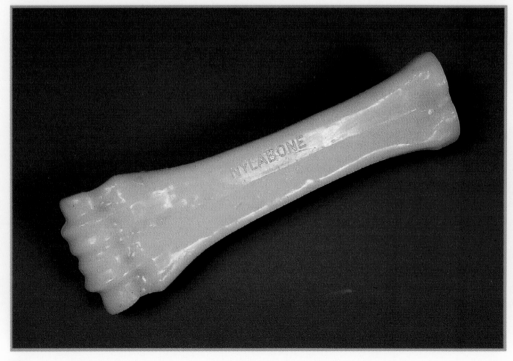

Roar-Hide® is completely edible and is high in protein (over 86%) and low in fat (less than one-third of 1%). Unlike common rawhide, it is safer, less messy, and more fun.

the sides. Due to the abrasive nature of these bones, they should be offered most sparingly. Knuckle bones, though once very popular for dogs, can be easily chewed up and eaten by dogs. At the very least, digestion is interrupted; at worst, the dog can choke or suffer from intestinal blockage.

When a dog chews hard on a Nylabone®, little bristle-like projections appear on the surface of the bone. These help to clean the dog's teeth and add to the gum-massaging. Given the chemistry of the nylon, the bristle can pass through the dog's intestinal tract without effect. Since nylon is inert, no microorganism can grow on it, and it can be washed in soap and water or sterilized in boiling water or in an autoclave.

For the sake of your dog, his teeth and your own peace of mind, provide your dog with Nylabones®. They have 100 variations from which to choose.

FIGHTING FLEAS

Fleas are very mobile and may be red, black, or brown in color. The adults suck the blood of the host, while the larvae feed on the feces of the adults, which is rich in blood. Flea "dirt" may be seen on the pup as very tiny clusters of blackish specks that look like freshly ground pepper. The eggs of fleas may be laid on the puppy, though they are more commonly laid off the host in a favorable place, such as the bedding.

They normally hatch in 4 to 21 days, depending on the temperature, but they can survive for up to 18 months if temperature conditions are not favorable. The larvae are maggot-like and molt a couple of times before forming pupae, which can survive long periods until the temperature, or the vibration of a nearby host, causes them to emerge and jump on a host.

There are a number of effective treatments available, and you should discuss them with your veterinarian, then follow all instructions for the one you choose. Any treatment will involve a product for your puppy or dog and one for the environment, and will require diligence on your part to treat all areas and thoroughly clean your home and yard until the infestation is eradicated.

THE TROUBLE WITH TICKS

Ticks are arthropods of the spider family, which means they have eight legs (though the larvae have six). They bury their headparts into the host and gorge on its blood. They are easily seen as small grain-like creatures sticking out from the skin. They are often picked up when dogs play in fields, but may also arrive in your yard via wild animals—even birds—or stray cats and dogs. Some ticks are species-specific, others are more adaptable and will host on many species.

Under ideal conditions, fleas can complete their life cycle in three weeks. Courtesy of Fleabusters, Rx for Fleas, Inc., Fort Lauderdale, Florida.

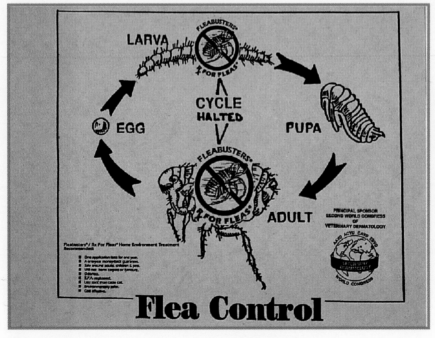

The deer tick is the most common carrier of Lyme disease. Photo courtesy of Virbac Laboratories, Inc., Fort Worth, Texas.

The most troublesome type of tick is the deer tick, which spreads the deadly Lyme disease that can cripple a dog (or a person). Deer ticks are tiny and very hard to detect. Often, by the time they're big enough to notice, they've been feeding on the dog for a few days—long enough to do their damage. Lyme disease was named for the area of the United States in which it was first detected—Lyme, Connecticut—but has now been diagnosed in almost all parts of the U.S. Your veterinarian can advise you of the danger to your dog(s) in your area, and may suggest your dog be vaccinated for Lyme. Always go over your dog with a fine-toothed flea comb when you come in from walking through any area that may harbor deer ticks, and if your dog is acting unusually sluggish or sore, seek veterinary advice.

Attempts to pull a tick free will invariably leave the headpart in the pup, where it will die and cause an infected wound or abscess. The best way to remove ticks is to dab a strong saline solution, iodine, or alcohol on them. This will numb them, causing them to loosen their hold, at which time they can be removed with forceps. The wound can then be cleaned and covered with an antiseptic ointment. If ticks are common in your area, consult with your vet for a suitable pesticide to be used in kennels, on bedding, and on the puppy or dog.

INSECTS AND OTHER OUTDOOR DANGERS

There are many biting insects, such as mosquitoes, that can cause discomfort to a puppy. Many diseases are transmitted by the males of these species.

A pup can easily get a grass seed or thorn lodged between his pads or in the folds of his ears. These may go unnoticed until an abscess forms.

This is where your daily check of the puppy or dog will do a world of good. If your puppy has been playing in long grass or places where there may be thorns,

pine needles, wild animals, or parasites, the check-up is a wise precaution.

Kuvasz puppies playing outdoors in the grass are subject to thorns, needles, and roaming critters. Always give your pup a thorough check-up after he has been playing outside.

SKIN DISORDERS

Apart from problems associated with lesions created by biting pests, a puppy may fall foul to a number of other skin disorders. Examples are ringworm, mange, and eczema. Ringworm is not caused by a worm, but is a fungal infection. It manifests itself as a sore-looking bald circle. If your puppy should have any form of bald patches, let your veterinarian check him over; a microscopic examination can confirm the condition. Many old remedies for ringworm exist, such as iodine, carbolic acid, formalin, and other tinctures, but modern drugs are superior.

Fungal infections can be very difficult to treat, and even more difficult to eradicate, because of the spores. These can withstand most treatments, other than burning, which is the best thing to do with bedding once the condition has been confirmed.

Mange is a general term that can be applied to many skin conditions where the hair falls out and a flaky crust develops and falls away.

Often, dogs will scratch themselves, and this invariably is worse than the original condition, for it opens lesions that are then subject to viral, fungal, or parasitic attack. The cause of the problem can be various species of mites. These either live on skin debris and the hair follicles, which they destroy, or they bury themselves just beneath the skin and feed on the tissue. Applying general remedies from pet stores is not recommended because it is essential to identify the type of mange before a specific treatment is effective.

Eczema is another non-specific term applied to many skin disorders. The condition can be brought about in many ways. Sunburn, chemicals, allergies to foods, drugs, pollens, and even stress can all produce a deterioration of the skin and coat. Given the range of causal factors, treatment can be difficult because the problem is one of identification. It is a case of taking each possibility at a time and trying to correctly diagnose the matter. If the cause is of a dietary nature then you must remove one item at a time in order to find out if the dog is allergic to a given food. It could, of course, be the lack of a nutrient that is the problem, so if the condition persists, you should consult your veterinarian.

INTERNAL DISORDERS

It cannot be overstressed that it is very foolish to attempt to diagnose an internal disorder without the advice of a veterinarian. Take a relatively common problem such as diarrhea. It might be caused by nothing more serious than the puppy hogging a lot of food or eating something that it has never previously eaten. Conversely, it could be the first indication of a potentially fatal disease. It's up to your veterinarian to make the correct diagnosis.

The following symptoms, especially if they accompany each other or are progressively added to earlier symptoms, mean you should visit the veterinarian right away:

Continual vomiting. All dogs vomit from time to time and this is not necessarily a sign of illness. They will eat grass to induce vomiting. It is a natural cleansing process common to many carnivores. However, continued vomiting is a clear sign of a problem. It may be a blockage in the pup's intestinal tract, it may be induced by worms, or it could be due to any number of diseases.

Diarrhea. This, too, may be nothing more than a temporary condition due to many factors. Even a change of home can induce diarrhea, because this often stresses the pup, and invariably there is some change in the diet. If it persists more than 48 hours then something is amiss. If blood is seen in the feces, waste no time at all in taking the dog to the vet.

Running eyes and/or nose. A pup might have a chill and this will cause the eyes and nose to weep. Again, this should quickly clear up if the puppy is placed in a warm environment and away from any drafts. If it does not, and especially if a mucous discharge is seen, then the pup has an illness that must be diagnosed.

Coughing. Prolonged coughing is a sign of a problem, usually of a respiratory nature.

Wheezing. If the pup has difficulty breathing and makes a wheezing sound when breathing, then something is wrong.

Cries when attempting to defecate or urinate. This might only be a minor problem due to the hard state of the feces, but it could be more serious, especially if the pup cries when urinating.

Cries when touched. Obviously, if you do not handle a puppy with care he might yelp. However, if he cries even when lifted gently, then he has an internal problem that becomes apparent when pressure is applied to a given area of the body. Clearly, this must be diagnosed.

Refuses food. Generally, puppies and dogs are greedy creatures when it comes to feeding time. Some might be more fussy, but none should refuse more than one meal. If they go for a number of hours without showing any interest in their food, then something is not as it should be.

General listlessness. All puppies have their off days when they do not seem their usual cheeky, mischievous selves. If this condition persists for more than two days then there is little doubt of a problem. They may not show any of the signs listed, other than perhaps a reduced interest in their food. There are many diseases that can develop internally without displaying obvious clinical signs. Blood, fecal, and other tests are needed in order to identify the disorder before it reaches an advanced state that may not be treatable.

WORMS

There are many species of worms, and a number of these live in the tissues of dogs and most other animals. Many create no problem at all, so you are not even aware they exist. Others can be tolerated in small levels, but become a major problem if they number more than a few. The most common types seen in dogs are roundworms and tapeworms. While roundworms are the greater problem, tapeworms require an intermediate host so are more easily eradicated.

Roundworms of the species *Toxocara canis* infest the dog. They may grow to a length of 8 inches (20 cm) and look like strings of spaghetti. The worms feed on the digesting food in the pup's intestines. In chronic cases the puppy will become pot-bellied, have diarrhea, and will vomit. Eventually, he will stop eating, having passed through the stage when he always seems hungry. The worms lay eggs in the puppy and these pass out in his feces. They are then either ingested by the pup, or they are eaten by mice, rats, or beetles. These may then be eaten by the puppy and the life cycle is complete.

Larval worms can migrate to the womb of a pregnant bitch, or to her mammary glands, and this is how they pass to the puppy. The pregnant bitch can be

Roundworms are spaghetti-like worms that cause a pot-bellied appearance and dull coat, along with more severe symptoms, such as diarrhea and vomiting. Photo courtesy of Merck AgVet.

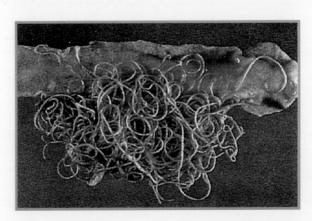

Whipworms are hard to find unless you strain your dog's feces, and this is best left to a veterinarian. Pictured here are adult whipworms.

wormed, which will help. The pups can, and should, be wormed when they are about two weeks old. Repeat worming every 10 to 14 days and the parasites should be removed. Worms can be extremely dangerous to young puppies, so you should be sure the pup is wormed as a matter of routine.

Tapeworms can be seen as tiny rice-like eggs sticking to the puppy's or dog's anus. They are less destructive, but still undesirable. The eggs are eaten by mice, fleas, rabbits, and other animals that serve as intermediate hosts. They develop into a larval stage and the host must be eaten by the dog in order to complete the chain. Your vet will supply a suitable remedy if tapeworms are seen or suspected. The vet can also do an egg count on the pup's feces under the microscope; this will indicate the extent of an infestation.

There are other worms, such as hookworms and whipworms, that are also blood suckers. They will make a pup anemic, and blood might be seen in the feces, which can be examined by the vet to confirm their presence. Cleanliness in all matters is the best preventative measure for all worms.

BLOAT (GASTRIC DILATATION)

This condition has proved fatal in many dogs, especially large and deep-chested breeds, such as the Weimaraner and the Great Dane. However, any dog can get bloat. It is caused by swallowing air during exercise, food/water gulping or another strenuous task. As many believe, it is not the result of flatulence. The stomach of an affected dog twists, disallowing food and blood flow and resulting in harmful toxins being released into the bloodstream. Death can easily follow if the condition goes undetected.

The best preventative measure is not to feed large meals or exercise your puppy or dog immediately after he has eaten. Veterinarians recommend feeding three smaller meals per day in an elevated feeding rack, adding water to dry food to prevent gulping, and not offering water during mealtimes.

VACCINATIONS

Every puppy, purebred or mixed breed, should be vaccinated against the major canine diseases. These are distemper, leptospirosis, hepatitis, and canine parvovirus. Your puppy may have received a temporary vaccination against distemper before you purchased him, but be sure to ask the breeder to be sure.

The age at which vaccinations are given can vary, but will usually be when the pup is 8 to 12 weeks old. By this time any protection given to the pup by antibodies received from his mother via her initial milk feeds will be losing their strength.

Rely on your veterinarian for the most effectual vaccination schedule for your Kuvasz puppy.

The puppy's immune system works on the basis that the white blood cells engulf and render harmless

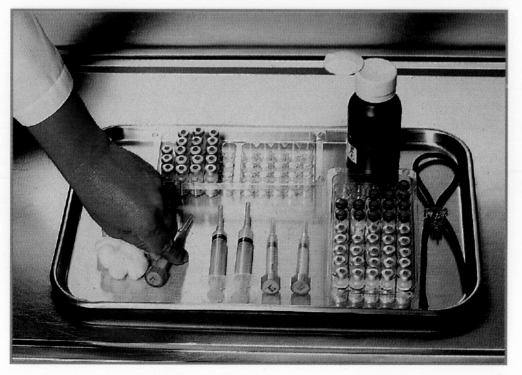

attacking bacteria. However, they must first recognize a potential enemy.

Vaccines are either dead bacteria or they are live, but in very small doses. Either type prompts the pup's defense system to attack them. When a large attack then comes (if it does), the immune system recognizes it and massive numbers of lymphocytes (white blood corpuscles) are mobilized to counter the attack. However, the ability of the cells to recognize these dangerous viruses can diminish over a period of time. It is therefore useful to provide annual reminders about the nature of the enemy. This is done by means of booster injections that keep the immune system on its alert. Immunization is not 100-percent guaranteed to be successful, but is very close. Certainly it is better than giving the puppy no protection.

Dogs are subject to other viral attacks, and if these are of a high-risk factor in your area, then your vet will suggest you have the puppy vaccinated against these as well.

Your puppy or dog should also be vaccinated against the deadly rabies virus. In fact, in many places it is illegal for your dog not to be vaccinated. This is to protect your dog, your family, and the rest of the animal population from this deadly virus that infects the nervous system and causes dementia and death.

ACCIDENTS

All puppies will get their share of bumps and bruises due to the rather energetic way they play. These will usually heal themselves over a few days. Small cuts should be bathed with a suitable disinfectant and then smeared with an antiseptic ointment. If a cut looks more serious, then stem the flow of blood with a towel or makeshift tourniquet and rush the pup to the veterinarian. Never apply so much pressure to the wound that it might restrict the flow of blood to the limb.

In the case of burns you should apply cold water or an ice pack to the surface. If the burn was due to a chemical, then this must be washed away with copious amounts of water. Apply petroleum jelly, or any vegetable oil, to the burn. Trim away the hair if need be. Wrap the dog in a blanket and rush him to the vet. The pup may go into shock, depending on the severity of the burn, and this will result in a lowered blood pressure, which is dangerous and the reason the pup must receive immediate veterinary attention.

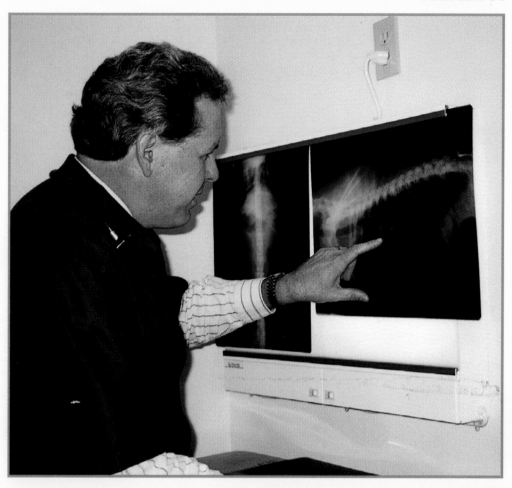

It is a good idea to x-ray the chest and abdomen on any dog hit by a car.

If a broken limb is suspected then try to keep the animal as still as possible. Wrap your pup or dog in a blanket to restrict movement and get him to the veterinarian as soon as possible. Do not move the dog's head so it is tilting backward, as this might result in blood entering the lungs.

Do not let your pup jump up and down from heights, as this can cause considerable shock to the joints. Like all youngsters, puppies do not know when enough is enough, so you must do all their thinking for them.

Provided you apply strict hygiene to all aspects of raising your puppy, and you make daily checks on his physical state, you have done as much as you can to safeguard him during his most vulnerable period. Routine visits to your veterinarian are also recommended, especially while the puppy is under one year of age. The vet may notice something that did not seem important to you.

CONGENITAL AND ACQUIRED DISORDERS

by Judy Iby, RVT

Veterinarians and breeders now recognize that many of the disease processes and faults in dogs, as well as in human beings, have a genetic predisposition. These faults are found not only in the purebred dog but in the mixed breed as well. In my opinion, these diseases have been present for decades but more recently are being identified and attributed to inheritance. Fortunately many of these problems are not life threatening or even debilitating. Many of these disorders have a low incidence. It is true that some breeds and some bloodlines within a breed have a higher frequency than others. It is always wise to discuss this subject with breeders of your breed.

Presently very few of the hundreds of disorders can be identified through genetic testing. Hopefully with today's technology and the desire to improve our breeding stock, genetic testing will become more readily available. In the meantime the reputable breeder does the recommended testing for his breed. The American Kennel Club is encouraging OFA (Orthopedic Foundation for Animals) hip and elbow certification and CERF (Canine Eye Registration Foundation) certifications and is listing them on AKC registrations and pedigrees. This is a step forward for the AKC in encouraging better breeding. They also founded a Canine Health Foundation to aid in the research of diseases in the purebred dog.

Opposite: The responsible Kuvasz breeder, understanding the potential problems within the breed, strives to produce healthy puppies and contribute to the betterment of the breed.

BONES AND JOINTS

Hip Dysplasia

Canine hip dysplasia has been confirmed in 79 breeds. It is the malformation of the hip joint's ball and socket, with clinical signs from none to severe hip lameness. It may appear as early as five months. The incidence is

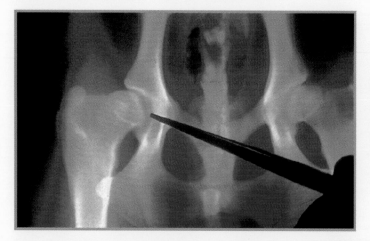

Radiograph of a dog with hip dysplasia. Note the flattened femoral head at the marker. Photo courtesy of Toronto Academy of Veterinary Medicine, Toronto, Canada.

reduced within a bloodline by breeding normal to normal, generation after generation. Upon submitting normal pelvic radiographs, the OFA will issue a certification number.

Elbow Dysplasia

Elbow dysplasia results from abnormal development of the ulna, one of the bones of the upper arm. During bone growth, a small area of bone (the anconeal process) fails to fuse with the rest of the bone. This results in an unstable elbow joint and lameness, which is aggravated by exercise. OFA certifies free of this disorder.

Patellar Luxation

This condition can be medial or lateral. Breeders call patellar luxations "slips" for "slipped stifles" and they may be unilateral or bilateral. OFA offers a registry for this disorder. Patellar luxations may or may not cause problems.

Intervertebral Disk Disease (IVD)

The degeneration is progressive, starting as early as two to nine months, but usually the neurological symptoms are not apparent until three to six years of age. Symptoms include pain, paresis (weariness), incoordination, and paralysis. IVD is a medical emergency. If you are unable to get professional care immediately, then confine your dog to a crate or small area until he can be seen.

Spondylitis

Usually seen in middle to old-age dogs and poten-

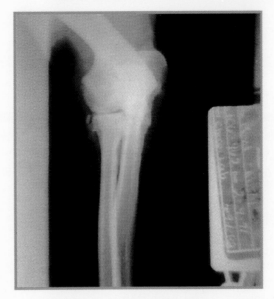

Fragmented coronoid process of the elbow, a manifestation of elbow dysplasia. Photo courtesy of Jack Henry.

tially quite serious in the latter, spondylitis is inflammation of the vertebral joints and degeneration of intervertebral disks resulting in bony spur-like outgrowths ventrally that may fuse.

Transitional Vertebrae

This congenital birth defect is found in some bloodlines. Usually the most common type is the sacralization of the seventh lumbar vertebra and seldom causes clinical signs. If the sacralization of the last lumbar vertebra is unilateral, then a tilt may be present in the pelvic axis, which can affect the dog's movement.

Over and Undershot Jaw

This occurs when there is abnormal relative growth of the mandible and/or maxilla. It is prevalent in some bloodlines.

CARDIOVASCULAR AND LYMPHATIC SYSTEMS

Dilated Cardiomyopathy

Prevalent in several breeds, this is a disease in which the heart muscle is damaged or destroyed to the point that it cannot pump blood properly through the body resulting in signs of heart failure. Diagnosis is confirmed by cardiac ultrasound.

Patent Ductus Arteriosus

At birth, a patent (open) ductus arteriosus results in

impaired circulation through the lungs and poor oxygenation of the blood. Since it has a poor prognosis, the puppy should be returned to the breeder.

Ventricular Septal Defect

Some dogs are asymptomatic and others may develop congestive heart failure during middle age. It is a heart defect found in young dogs in which there is an opening in the septum that separates the left ventricle from the right ventricle.

Sick Sinus Syndrome

Sick sinus syndrome is a complex of arrhythmias that predisposes the animal to hypotension, weakness, and syncope (fainting). It is rarely fatal but the dog may require a pacemaker. Pacemakers are becoming more common in dogs.

Lymphosarcoma

This condition can occur in young dogs but usually appears in dogs over the age of five years. Symptoms include fever, weight loss, anorexia, painless enlargement of the lymph nodes, and nonspecific signs of illness. It is the most common type of cancer found in dogs. Chemotherapy treatment will prolong the dog's life but will not cure the disease at this time.

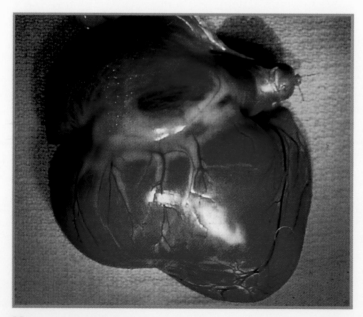

Possibly a congenital disorder, dilated cardiomyopathy is marked by a "swollen" condition in which the heart muscle becomes thin and stretched. Photo courtesy of Dr. Kenneth Jeffery, Mesa, Arizona.

BLOOD

Von Willebrand's Disease

VWD has been confirmed in over 50 breeds and is a manageable disease. It is characterized by moderate to severe bleeding, corrected by blood transfusions from normal dogs and frequently seen with hypothyroidism. When levels are low, a pre-surgical blood transfusion may be necessary. Many breeders screen their breeding stock for vWD.

Immune-Mediated Blood Disease

Immune-mediated diseases affect the red blood cells and platelets. They are called autoimmune hemolytic anemia or immune-mediated anemia when red blood cells are affected, and autoimmune thrombocytopenic purpura, idiopathic throm-bocytopenic purpura, and immune-mediated thrombocytopenia when platelets are involved. The disease may appear acutely. Symptoms include jaundice (yellow color) of the gums and eyes and dark brown or dark red urine. Symptoms of platelet disease include pinpoint bruises or hemorrhages in the skin, gums and eye membranes; nosebleeds; bleeding from the GI tract or into the urine. Any of these symptoms constitutes an emergency!

DIGESTIVE SYSTEM AND ORAL CAVITY

Megaesophagus

This may be acquired later in life but usually appears in young puppies after weaning. The esophagus enlarges and cannot properly propel food from the throat into the stomach. Elevating the food helps. A complication of megaesophagus is pneumonia, which results from inhaling pieces of food.

Tonsil Enlargement

The tonsils should be in their crypts, not visible.

Oral Fibrosarcoma and Melanoma

Fibrosarcomas are malignant, and the majority of melanomas of the mouth are also malignant.

Colitis

This disorder may be idiopathic (no known cause) and appears with some frequency in bloodlines. It is characterized by an intermittent bloody stool, with or without diarrhea.

Chronic Hepatitis

This is the result of liver failure occuring at relatively young ages. In many cases clinical signs are apparent for less than two weeks. They include anorexia, lethargy, vomiting, depression, diarrhea, trembling or shaking, polydipsia/polyuria, weight loss, and melena (dark bloody stool). Early diagnosis and treatment promise the best chance for survival.

Copper Toxicity

Copper toxicity occurs when excessive copper is concentrated in the liver. In 1995 there was a breakthrough when the DNA marker was identified in one of the afflicted breeds. Therefore carriers will be identified in the future.

ENDOCRINE SYSTEM

Hypothyroidism

Over 50 breeds have been diagnosed with hypothyroidism. It is the number-one endocrine disorder in the dog and is the result of an underactive thyroid gland. Conscientious breeders are screening their dogs if the disease is common to their breed or bloodline. The critical years for the decline of thyroid function are usually between three and eight, although it can appear at an older age. A simple blood test can diagnose or rule out this disorder. It is easily and inexpensively treated by giving thyroid-replacement therapy daily. Untreated hypothyroidism can be devastating to your dog.

Listed below are some of the symptoms but please remember these signs can be related to a disease other than hypothyroidism.

Alterations in Cellular Metabolism: lethargy, mental dullness, exercise intolerance, neurologic signs (polyneuropathy, seizures), weight gain, cold intolerance, mood swings, hyperexcitability, stunted growth, and chronic infections. Some behavioral problems have been attributed to hypothyroidism.

Hematologic: bleeding, bone marrow failure, low red blood cell count (anemia), low white blood cell count, and low platelet count.

Ocular Disorders: corneal lipid deposits, corneal ulceration, uveitis, keratoconjunctivitis (dry eye), and infections of eyelid gland (meibomian gland).

Neuromuscular Problems: weakness, stiffness, laryngeal paralysis, facial paralysis, "tragic expression," knuckling or dragging feet, muscle wasting, megaesophagus, head tilt, and drooping eyelids.

Dermatologic Diseases: dry, scaly skin and dandruff, coarse, dull coat, bilaterally symmetrical hair loss, "rat tail," "puppy coat," hyperpigmentation, nasodigital hyperkeratosis, seborrhea, greasy skin, pyoderma or skin infections, myxedema, chronic offensive skin odor, and chronic ear infections.

Cardiac Abnormalities: slow heart rate (bradycardia), cardia arrhythmias, and dilated cardiomyopathy.

Gastrointestinal Disorders: constipation, diarrhea, and vomiting.

Reproductive Disorders: infertility of either sex, lack of libido, testicular atrophy, hypospermia, aspermia, prolonged interestrous interval, absence of heat cycles, silent heats, pseudopregnancy, weak, dying or stillborn puppies.

Addison's Disease

Primary adrenal insufficiency is caused by damage to the adrenal cortex, and secondary adrenocortical insufficiency is the result of insufficient production of the hormone ACTH by the pituitary gland. Symptoms may include depression, anorexia, a weak femoral pulse, vomiting or diarrhea, weakness, dehydration, and occasionally bradycardia.

Cushing's Disease

Hyperadrenocorticism is the over-production of glucocorticoid. Dogs on steroid therapy may show Cushing-like symptoms. Some of the symptoms are polydipsia, polyuria, nonpruritic alopecia, and an enlarged, pendulous, or flaccid abdomen.

EYES

Cataracts

Breeders should screen their breeding stock for this disorder. A cataract is defined as any opacity of the lens or its capsule. It may progress and produce blindness or it may remain small and cause no clinical impairment of vision. Unfortunately some inherited cataracts appear later in life after the dog has already been bred.

Lens Luxation

This condition results when the lens of the eye is not in normal position, and may result in secondary glaucoma.

Lens Induced Uveitis

Lens induced uveitis is an inflammation in the eye resulting from leakage of lens protein through the capsule, most frequently seen in rapidly developing cataracts.

Glaucoma, Primary

Primary glaucoma is caused by increased intraocular pressure due to inadequate aqueous drainage and is not associated with other intraocular diseases. It may initially be in one eye.

Glaucoma, Secondary

Secondary glaucoma is caused by increased intraocular pressure brought on by another ocular disease, tumor, or inflammation.

Keratoconjunctivitis Sicca

"Dry eye" (the decrease in production of tears) may be the result of a congenital or inherited deficiency of the aqueous layer, a lack of the proper nervous stimulation of the tearing system, a traumatic incident, or drugs, including topical anesthetics (such as atropine, and antibiotics containing sulfadiazine, phenazopyridine or salicyla-sulfapyridine). Additional causes include immune-mediated disease and other assorted illnesses. There seems to be an increased incidence of "dry eye" after "cherry eye" removal.

Progressive Retinal Atrophy (PRA)

This is the progressive loss of vision, first at night, followed by total blindness. It is inherited in many breeds. The defective gene has been identified in at least one of those breeds.

Distichiasis

Distichiasis results from extra rows of eyelashes growing out of the meibomian gland ducts. This condition may cause tearing, but tearing may be the result of some other problem that needs to be investigated.

Entropion

Entropion is the inward rolling of the eyelid, usually lower lid, which can cause inflammation and may need surgical correction.

Ectropion

Ectropion is the outward rolling of the eyelid, usually lower lid, and may need surgical correction.

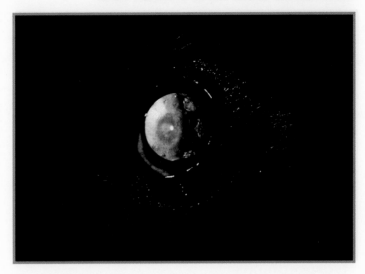

An immature cataract is evident in this dilated pupil. The central white area and cloudy areas at 4:00, 6:00 and 8:00 represent the cataract. Photo courtesy of Dr. Kerry L. Ketring.

Nasolacrimal Puncta Atresia

A common problem in some breeds is a closed tear duct, which may need to be professionally opened.

Hypertrophy of the Nictitans Gland

"Cherry eye" is the increase in size of the gland resulting in eversion of the third eyelid and is usually bilateral. Onset frequently occurs during stressful periods such as teething.

Facial Paralysis

Clinical signs include drooped ear, paralyzed eyelid, and drooped lip with possible drooling or food collection. Eventually the muscles atrophy and the lip and ear may be pulled up. It can be unilateral or bilateral. The dog may not be able to blink but may be able to compensate by retracting the eye inward. The condition runs in some bloodlines, but it may be the result of hypothyroidism or a middle-ear infection. It is not a stroke.

NEUROMUSCULAR SYSTEM

Epilepsy

Epilepsy is a disorder in which the electrical brain activity "short circuits," resulting in a seizure. Numerous breeds and mixed breeds are subject to idiopathic epilepsy (no explainable reason). Seizures usually begin between six months and five years of age. Don't panic. Your primary concern should be to keep your dog from hurting himself by falling down the stairs or falling off furniture and/or banging his head. Dogs don't swallow their tongues. If the seizure lasts longer than ten minutes, you should contact your veterinarian. Seizures can be caused by many conditions, such as poisoning and birth injuries, brain infections, trauma or tumors, liver disease, distemper, and low blood sugar or calcium. There are all types of seizures from generalized (the dog will be shaking and paddling/kicking his feet) to standing and staring out in space, etc.

Behavioral Abnormalities

These include aggression, timidness, fear of noise, and abnormal maternal behavior.

Hydrocephalus

This disorder is characterized by excessive accumulation of cerebrospinal fluid. The skull enlarges to accommodate the additional fluid. Neurological disorders may be observed. Not all cases are inherited.

SKIN

Seborrhea

This is a condition recognized in several breeds. The skin cells and sebum are being overproduced. There is a defect in the skin and sebaceous gland cells. Affected dogs are born with this defect.

Atopy

Atopy is the medical term referring to inhalant allergies. Commonly inhaled allergens include weed, grass and tree pollens, mold, housedust, and housedust mites. Signs include licking of the feet, scratching of the trunk, and rubbing of the muzzle. Allergy vaccines can be prepared with the aid of intradermal (skin) testing. A less effective method of testing is the blood allergy test.

Food Allergy

Dogs with a food allergy frequently show signs of severe itching and scratching. The itching and scratching may be localized or generalized. Food allergy may result in recurrent bacterial skin and ear infections. Feeding a restricted diet is the most accurate method of diagnosing food allergy for a period of four to ten weeks. Recurrence of the